teacher's friend publications

October

a creative idea book
for the
elementary teacher

written and illustrated
by
Karen Sevaly

Copyright © 1991
Teacher's Friend Publications, Inc.
All rights reserved.
Printed in the United States of America
Published by Teacher's Friend Publications, Inc.
3240 Trade Center Dr., Riverside, CA 92507

ISBN-0-943263-01-8

TO TEACHERS AND CHILDREN EVERYWHERE.

Table of Contents

Making the Most of It!

WHAT IS IN
THIS BOOK:

You will find the following in each monthly idea book from Teachers Friend Publications:

1. A calendar listing every day of the month with a classroom idea.

2. At least four new student awards to be sent home to parents.

3. Three new bookmarks that can be used in your school library or given to students by you as "Super Student Awards."

4. Numerous bulletin board ideas and patterns pertaining to the particular month.

5. Easy to make craft ideas related to the monthly holidays.

6. Dozens of activities emphasizing not only the obvious holidays but also chapters related to such subjects as; Dinosaurs and Fire Safety.

7. Crossword puzzles, word finds, creative writing pages, booklet covers and much more.

8. Scores of classroom management techniques, the newest and the best.

HOW TO USE
THIS BOOK:

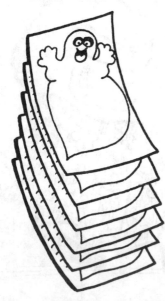

Every page of this book may be duplicated for individual classroom use.

Some pages are meant to be used as duplicating masters and used as student work sheets. Other pages may be copied onto construction paper or used as they are.

If you have access to a print shop, you will find that many pages work well when printed on index paper. This type of paper takes crayons and felt markers well and is sturdy enough to last and last. The wheel pattern and bookmarks are two items that work particularly well on index paper.

Lastly, some pages are meant to be enlarged with an overhead or opaque projector. When we say enlarge, we mean it! Think BIG! Three, four or even five feet is great! Try using colored butcher paper or poster board so you don't spend all your time coloring.

OCTOBER

Making the Most of It!

ADDING THE COLOR:

Putting the color to finished items can be a real bother to teachers in a rush. Try these ideas:

1. On small areas, water color markers work great. If your area is rather large switch to crayons or even colored chalk or pastels.

   (Don't worry, lamination or a spray fixative will keep the color on the work and off of you. No laminator or fixative? That's okay, a little hair spray will do the trick.)

2. The quickest method of coloring large items is to simply start with colored paper. (Poster board, butcher paper and large construction paper work well.) Add a few dashes of a contrasting colored marker or crayon and you will have it made.

3. Try cutting character eyes, teeth, etc. from white typing paper and gluing them in place. These features will really stand out and make your bulletin boards come alive.

   For special effects add real buttons or lace. Metallic paper looks great on stars and belt buckles, too.

LAMINATORS:

If you have access to a roll laminator you already know how fortunate you are. They are priceless when it comes to saving time and money. Try these ideas:

1. You can laminate more than just classroom posters and construction paper. Try various kinds of fabric, wall paper and gift wrapping. You'll be surprised at the great combinations you come up with.

   Laminated classified ads can be used to cut headings for current event bulletin boards. Colorful gingham fabric makes terrific cut letters or scalloped edging. You might even try burlap! It looks terrific on a fall bulletin board.

   (You can even make professional looking bookmarks with laminated fabric or burlap. They are great gift ideas.)

2. Felt markers and laminated paper or fabric can work as a team. Just make sure the markers you use are permanent and not water based. Oops, make a mistake! That's okay. Put a little ditto fluid on a tissue, rub across the mark and presto, it's gone! (Dry transfer markers work great on lamination, too.)

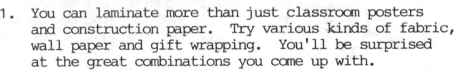

Making the Most of It!

LAMINATORS:
(continued)

3. Laminating cut-out characters can be tricky. If you have enlarged an illustration onto poster board, simply laminate first and then cut it out with an art knife. (Just make sure the laminator is plenty hot.)

One problem may arise when you paste an illustration onto poster board and laminate the finished product. If your paste-up does not cover 100% of the illustration, the poster board may separate from it after laminating. To avoid this problem, paste your illustration onto poster board that measures slightly larger. This way, the lamination will help hold down your illustration.

4. Have you ever laminated student-made place mats, crayon shavings, tissue paper collages, or dried flowers? You'll be amazed at the variety of creative things that can be laminated and used in the classroom, or as take-home gifts.

DITTO MASTERS:

Many of the pages in this book can be made into masters for duplicating. Try some of these ideas for best results:

1. When using new masters, turn down the pressure on the duplicating machine. As the copies become light, increase the pressure. This will get longer wear out of both the master and the machine.

2. If the print from the back side of your original comes through the front when making a master or photocopy, slip a sheet of black construction paper behind the sheet. This will mask the unwanted black lines and create a much better copy.

3. Trying to squeeze one more run out of that worn master can be frustrating. Try lightly spraying the inked side of the master with hair spray. For some reason, this helps the master put out those few extra copies.

4. Several potential masters in this book contain instructions for the teacher. Simply cover the type with correction fluid or a small slip of paper before duplicating.

Making the Most of It!

BULLETIN BOARDS:

Creating clever bulletin boards for your classroom need not take fantastic amounts of time and money. With a little preparation and know-how you can have different boards each month with very little effort. Try some of these ideas:

1. Background paper should be put up only once a year. Choose colors that can go with many themes and holidays. A black butcher paper background will look terrific with springtime butterflies or a spooky Halloween display.

2. Butcher paper is not the only thing that can be used to cover the back of your board. You might like to try the classified ad section of the local newspaper for a current events board. Or how about colored burlap? Just fold it up at the end of the year to reuse again.

3. Wallpaper is another great background cover. Discontinued rolls can be purchased for next to nothing at discount hardware stores. Most can be wiped clean and will not fade like construction paper. (Do not glue wallpaper directly to the board, just staple or pin in place.)

ON-GOING
BULLETIN BOARDS:

Creating the on-going bulletin board can be easy. Give one of these ideas a try.

1. Choose one board to be a calendar display. Students can change this monthly. They can do the switching of dates, month titles and holiday symbols. Start the year with a great calendar board and with a few minor changes each month it will add a sparkle to the classroom.

2. A classroom tree bulletin board is another one that requires very little attention after September. Cut a large bare tree from brown butcher paper and display it in the center of the board. (Wood-grained adhesive paper makes a great tree, also.) Children can add fall leaves, flowers, apples, Christmas ornaments, birds, valentines, etc., to change the appearance each month.

ON-GOING
BULLETIN BOARDS:
(continued)

3. Birthday bulletin boards, classroom helpers, school announcement displays and reading group charts can all be created once before school starts and changed monthly with very little effort. With all these on-going ideas, you'll discover that all that bulletin board space seems smaller than you thought.

LETTERING AND
HEADINGS:

Not every school has a letter machine that produces perfect 2" or 4" letters from construction paper. (There is such a thing, you know.) The rest of us will just have to use the old stencil and scissor method. But wait, there is an easier way!

1. Don't cut individual letters. They are difficult to pin up straight, anyway. Instead, hand print bulletin board titles and headings onto strips of colored paper. When it is time for the board to come down, simply roll it up to use again next year.

Use your imagination. Try cloud shapes and cartoon bubbles. They will all look great.

2. Hand lettering is not that difficult, even if your printing is not up to penmanship standards. Print block letters with a felt marker. Draw big dots at the ends of each letter. This will hide any mistakes and add a charming touch to the overall effect.

Calendar

- OCTOBER CALENDAR AND ACTIVITIES

- CALENDAR TOPPER

- BLANK CALENDAR

October

1   The first WORLD SERIES was played on this day in 1903. (Ask class baseball fans to report the latest in baseball news.)

2   MOHANDAS GANDHI, known as the "Father of India," was born on this day in 1869. (Describe Gandhi's devotion to non-violent reform to your students.)

3   Today is CHILD HEALTH DAY. (Ask students to list twelve ways in which they can help in keeping themselves healthy.)

4   The U.S.S.R. launched the first man-made satellite, SPUTNIC, on this day in 1957. (Gather a collection of space exploration books from the school library for your students to read.)

5   CHESTER A. ARTHUR, the 21st president of the United States, was born on this day in 1830. (Have students find out how many presidents we have had since Arthur.)

6   Today is UNIVERSAL CHILDREN'S DAY. (Celebrate the occasion by reading a special story or providing a treat for your students.)

7   Today is the DAY OF BREAD. (Discuss good nutrition with your class and have them sample different types of bread such as, tortillas, pita bread and bagels.)

8   Today is the birthdate of American political and religious leader, JESSE JACKSON, born in 1941. (Ask students to tell you the age of Mr. Jackson.)

9   Today is FIRE PREVENTION DAY. (Ask students to discuss fire safety with their parents and plan a family escape route in case of a fire in their home.)

10   The people of FIJI celebrate their independence on this day. The nation of Fiji includes 300 separate islands. (Ask your students to locate them on the classroom map.)

October

11 ELEANOR ROOSEVELT, American first lady and humanitarian, was born on this day in 1884. (Ask older students to find out why this particular first lady was so popular.)

12 Today is COLUMBUS DAY. This famous Italian explorer first sighted land on this day in 1492. (Have students trace his route from Spain to the West Indies on the classroom map.)

13 The UNITED STATES NAVY was established on this day in 1775. (Boys, in particular, might like to research various naval vessels and their impact throughout our history.)

14 The NOBEL PEACE PRIZE was awarded to Dr. Martin Luther King, Jr. on this day in 1964. (Ask students to find out about this award and how the recipients are chosen.)

15 Today is WORLD POETRY DAY. (Have students create their own original poems. Submit the best ones to the school newspaper.)

16 NOAH WEBSTER, creator of the American dictionary, was born on this day in 1758. (Give students five "haunting" words to locate in the class dictionary.)

17 Today, BLACK POETRY DAY, marks the birthdate of JUPITER HAMMON in 1711. He was the first published American black poet. (Find one of his poems and share it with your class.)

18 American inventor SAMUAL MORSE laid the first telegraph cable on this day in 1842. (Have students learn to signal their names in Morse Code.)

19 Today is YORKTOWN DAY. On this day in 1781, the last battle of the American Revolutionary War was fought. (Ask students to find Yorktown on the class map.)

20 RINGLING BROTHERS AND BARNUM AND BAILEY CIRCUS presented "The Greatest Show On Earth" for the first time on this day in 1919. (Ask students to write a short paper about their favorite circus act.)

21 THOMAS ALVA EDISON invented the first electric light on this day in 1879. (Have students research other Edison inventions.

22 FRANZ VON LISZT, the famous Hungarian pianist and composer, was born on this day in 1811. (In celebration, soothe your students with quiet classical music during free reading.)

October

23   The first NATIONAL WOMEN'S RIGHTS CONVENTION was held on this day in 1850. (Ask students to describe how women's rights have changed since then.)

24   The official establishment of the UNITED NATIONS was formed on this day in 1945. (Have students select a member nation and make it's flag from construction paper. Display the flags on the class bulletin board.)

25   RICHARD BYRD, famous American explorer, was born on this day in 1888. (Have students research his discovery and locate the route of his expedition on the class map.)

26   Today is INTERNATIONAL RED CROSS DAY. (Arrange for a Red Cross volunteer to visit your classroom and discuss the various services provided by this wonderful organization.

27   THEODORE ROOSEVELT, the 26th United States President, was born on this day in 1858. (Ask students to locate statistical information about the president, such as years served, place of birth and age at death.)

28   The STATUE OF LIBERTY was given to the United States by France on this day in 1886. (Ask students to bring in pictures and information about the statue and make a "Liberty" display on the class bulletin board.)

29   The countrymen of TURKEY celebrate their national independence which was proclaimed on this day in 1923. (Ask students to locate Turkey on the classroom map.)

30   JOHN ADAMS, 2nd United States President, was born on this day in 1735. (Ask students which president preceded Adams and which came after him.)

31   Today is HALLOWEEN! (Remind all of your witches, ghosts and goblins about being safe on Halloween.)

Calendar Topper

OCTOBER

October

sun	mon	tue	wed	thu	fri	sat

Autumn Activities

- PUMPKIN BOOK

- CREATIVE WRITING PAGE

- AUTUMN LEAVES

- BOOKMARKS

- AWARDS

- PENCIL TOPPERS

- CERTIFICATES

- COLOR PAGE

OCTOBER

Autumn Activities

Autumn is the time of year when leaves turn shades of yellow, orange and red, before softly falling to the ground. The sun sets earlier each evening and a sudden chill in the air tells us that winter is just around the corner. Winds play havoc with our hair and storm clouds grow dark and gray. It's time for birds to fly south and pumpkins to ripen in the fields. It's a magic time. A time when we all discover nature's beauty.

Bring this colorful season of autumn into your classroom by having your students enjoy some of these many activities.

"Maple"
"Oak"
"Sycamore"

TREE TALK

Discuss these autumn questions with your students.

What type of trees lose their leaves?

What are the names of some of these trees?

What trees lose their leaves near your home? On the school ground?

How does a tree use it's leaves?

How do animals and birds use the leaves?

LEAF STUDY

Collect enough large autumn leaves for everyone in class. Pass out one to each student. Draw a large leaf on the chalk board and label it's parts. Ask students to find these areas on their own leaves as you point them out on the board.

BLADE - broad part of the leaf containing the food making cells

VEINS - tiny network that moves the food product

PETIOLE - (stem) narrow channel that carries the food product to the tree

STIPULE - part of the stem that attaches to the tree

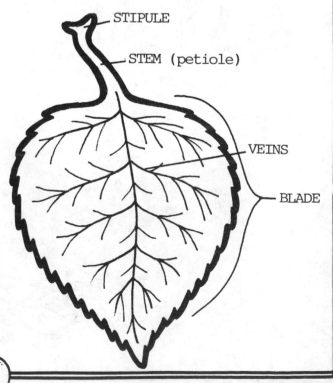

STIPULE

STEM (petiole)

VEINS

BLADE

Autumn Activities

LASTING LEAVES

Children will love to preserve their leaves by pressing them between sheets of waxed paper. Lay several thicknesses of newspaper on a table. Place the leaf or leaves between two sheets of waxed paper and cover with more newspaper. Press with a warm iron. (Laminating autumn leaves is also very successful.) Hang the lasting leaves in a sunny window for everyone to see.

LEAF RUBBINGS

Ask each student to place his or her leaf on the desk and cover it with a piece of smooth paper.

Using the side of a crayon, children gently rub across the leaf. Ask them to move their leaf and rub again, using a different color. Students can continue rubbing with different colors, even overlapping at times.

Display the rubbings on the class bulletin board or make booklet covers or autumn notebooks.

LEAF PAINTINGS

Primary children love to paint large, splashy abstract pictures. Give the students autumn colored tempera paint and let them paint boldly on construction paper. When the paintings are dry, trace a large leaf pattern over the paintings using a poster board stencil. Cut the leaves out and glue them to sheets of colored construction paper. Laminate if you wish or display them as they are.

Autumn Activities

LEAF STAMPS

Fall leaves make wonderful stamps for printing autumn designs. Mix autumn colors of tempera paint and ask children to gently coat one side of a leaf with the paint. Have them lay the leaf, paint side down, on a sheet of construction paper. Lift the leaf off the paper and repeat the process. The children can use one color of paint or several.

HARVEST COLLECTIONS

Ask students to collect a variety of nature's products for a class harvest display. Children will love collecting acorns, leaves, Indian corn, nuts, gourds and pumpkins. Arrange the items on a table top or in a large wicker basket. You might like to donate the display to the school office or cafeteria.

PUMPKIN FUN

Pass several small pumpkins around the classroom and ask students to examine the size, shape, texture and color of each one. Ask them to write about the pumpkins in their "Pumpkin Books" and draw detailed pictures.

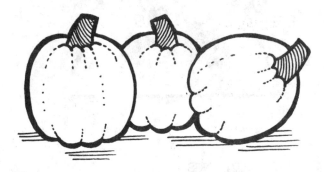

PUMPKIN SEEDS

Cut the top off one of the pumpkins while your students look on. Ask a few students to separate the seeds from the pulp. Place the seeds on a greased cookie sheet and sprinkle with salt. Roast at 350° until the seeds start to brown. Pass out a few to each student to enjoy.

Autumn Activities

PUMPKIN PLANTS

Save pumpkin seeds for planting later in the year. Dry the seeds on waxed paper and keep them in a small airtight container until spring.

When warm weather finally comes, give each student a small baby food jar or pint-sized milk carton. Have the students fill the containers with soil and plant two or three pumpkin seeds. Place the containers in a sunny window and keep the soil only slightly moist. After a few weeks, each pumpkin plant will be large enough to take home to mom for a Mother's Day gift.

PUMPKIN PUDDING

Cut the pumpkin into quarters and wrap in foil. Place in a pan and bake in the oven at 375° for about one hour. When the pumpkin has cooled, remove the outside skin and puree the pulp in an electric blender. Have the children take turns mixing the following ingredients:

3 cups of cooked pumpkin
2 beaten eggs
$1\frac{1}{2}$ cups of milk
1 cup of sugar
2 t. cinnamon
$\frac{1}{2}$ t. ginger
$\frac{1}{4}$ t. cloves
$\frac{1}{4}$ t. nutmeg
dash of salt

Cook the pudding in a saucepan for about 20 minutes. Continue stirring for best results. Serve the pudding in small paper cups when cool.

PUMPKIN PARTY

Serve pumpkin pudding with whipped cream and pumpkin seeds to your class as an extra special treat. While the children are enjoying their pumpkin feast, read the story of "Cinderella" or their own pumpkin stories in their "Pumpkin Books."

Pumpkin Book

Copy this pattern onto a folded sheet of construction paper. Place lined writing paper inside. Cut all layers of paper at one time. Staple at the fold.

Students may write their own "Pumpkin" stories inside.

Creative Writing

DRAW FACES ON THESE PUMPKINS AND WRITE A STORY ABOUT THEIR LIFE IN A PUMPKIN PATCH.

OCTOBER

Autumn Leaves

Use these fall patterns as bulletin board accents or name tags.

NO BONES ABOUT IT!

READING IS FUN!

GET ON TOP!

VISIT THE LIBRARY!

FLY AWAY WITH BOOKS...

READING IS BEWITCHING

_____ Name

FANG-TASTIC JOB!

REALLY DID A GREAT JOB TODAY!

Name

Teacher _____ Date

WAS A HUGE SUCCESS TODAY!

Date _____

Name

WAS BEWITCHING TODAY!

Teacher _____ Date

Pencil Toppers

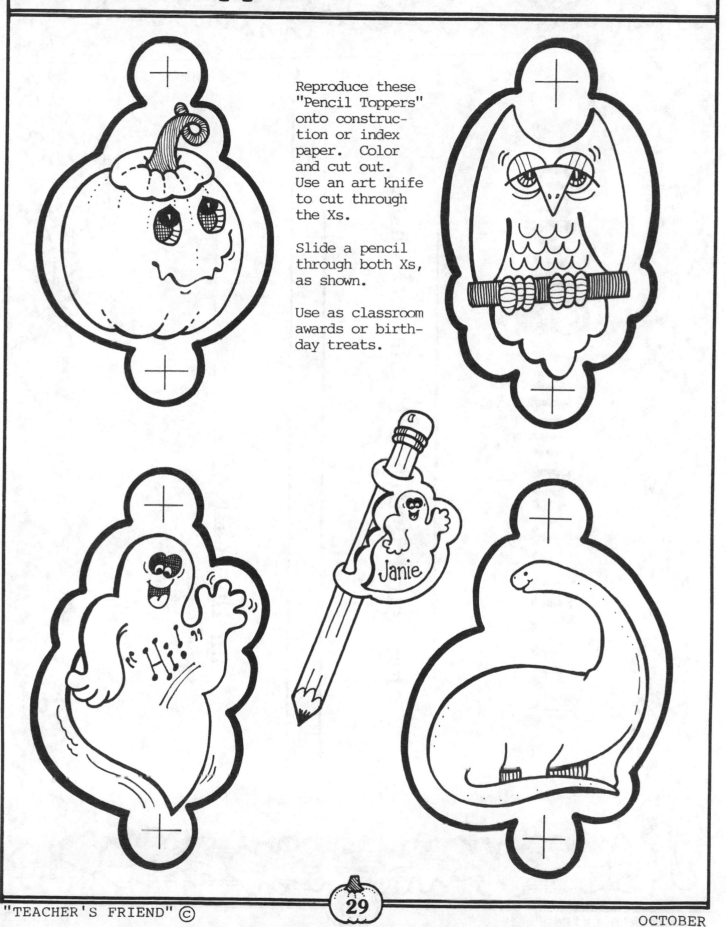

Reproduce these "Pencil Toppers" onto construction or index paper. Color and cut out. Use an art knife to cut through the Xs.

Slide a pencil through both Xs, as shown.

Use as classroom awards or birthday treats.

Janie

Participation Award

has participated with distinction in

_____

_____

_____

on this date, _____

_____
Principal

_____
Teacher

CERTIFICATE OF Recognition

This award of distinction is presented to

_____

in recognition of

_____

_____
date

Color Page

DRAW YOUR OWN
JACK-O'-LANTERN
FACES!

Dinosaurs

- DINOSAUR CROSSWORD

- DINOSAUR CARDS

- CREATIVE WRITING PAGE

- DINOSAUR PATTERNS

OCTOBER

Dinosaurs

Dinosaurs ruled the earth for nearly 100 million years. Scientists have learned about dinosaurs in many ways including the discovery of fossils, bones and eggs.

All dinosaurs were reptiles. The word "dinosaur" means "terrible lizard." Some of the giant dinosaurs could easily be described in these terms, but many of them were really rather small in size. Some dinosaurs walked on two feet while others walked on all four. Some were strictly plant eaters and others fierce meat eaters. Some dinosaurs preferred living in or near the water while still others preferred drier climates. One type of dinosaur, the pterodactyl, even flew like a bird.

Scientists are still puzzled over why the dinosaurs disappeared. Many believe that the earth slowly changed from moist warm areas to hot dry regions. This process caused a change in climate and effected the food supply. With plants and water diminishing, the dinosaurs soon died out.

Other scientists believe that this change in the earth's climate was caused by a great event such as a comet or asteroid crashing into the earth. Such an event would have caused a great dust cloud to form in the sky, blocking out the sunlight. With no sunlight, plants soon died and eventually the dinosaurs.

RESEARCH ACTIVITIES

1. Scientists that study fossils are called paleontologists. How do they know where to look for fossils? What type of tools do they use? Draw examples of at least three different fossils a paleontologist might find.

2. Scientists do not really know why the dinosaurs disappeared. Find out what most scientists believe about the changes in the earth and what may have caused the change. What evidence do they have? Write a short paper about these ideas.

3. On a world map, label the places where dinosaur bones have been found. Where have most of the bones been found? Is there a distinct pattern? If so, why? Is there a continent where dinosaur fossils have not been found?

4. Make a list of six dinosaurs. Tell whether they were meat-eaters or plant-eaters. List their approximate size. List a special fact about each dinosaur.

Dinosaur Crossword

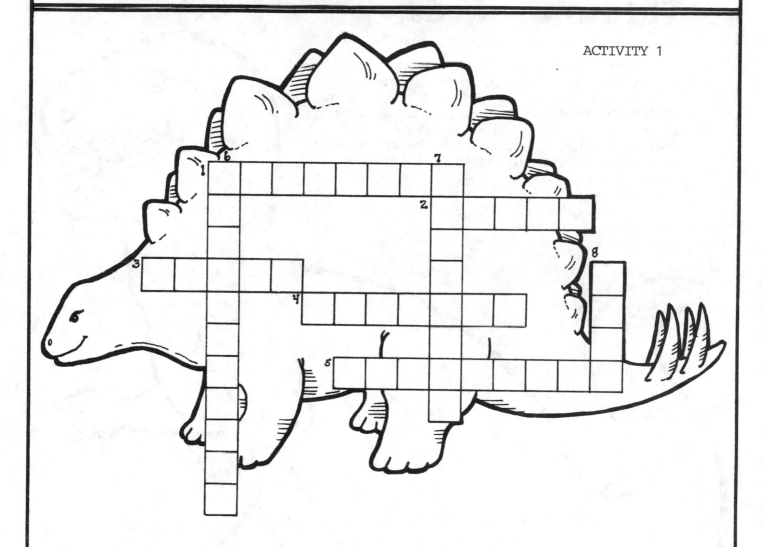

ACROSS

1. A giant reptile that lived millions of years ago.

2. Our planet.

3. The Stegosaurus was a _____-eater.

4. Ancient remains of plants or animals

5. A person that studies dinosaurs.

DOWN

6. Scientists are puzzled over why the dinosaurs _____.

7. All dinosaurs were _____.

8. The Tyrannosaurus was a _____-eater.

Tyrannosaurus

The Tyrannosaurus was the most ferocious of all the dinosaurs. He was a meat-eater with strong jaws and long, sharp teeth. He walked on his back legs and measured about 45 feet tall. The Tyrannosaurus is often called the "King" of the dinosaurs.

OCTOBER

Stegosaurus

The Stegosaurus was a plant-eating dinosaur about 18 feet long. He had a small head and large body with bony plates down his back. These plates and the spines on his tail helped protect the Stegosaurus from his enemies.

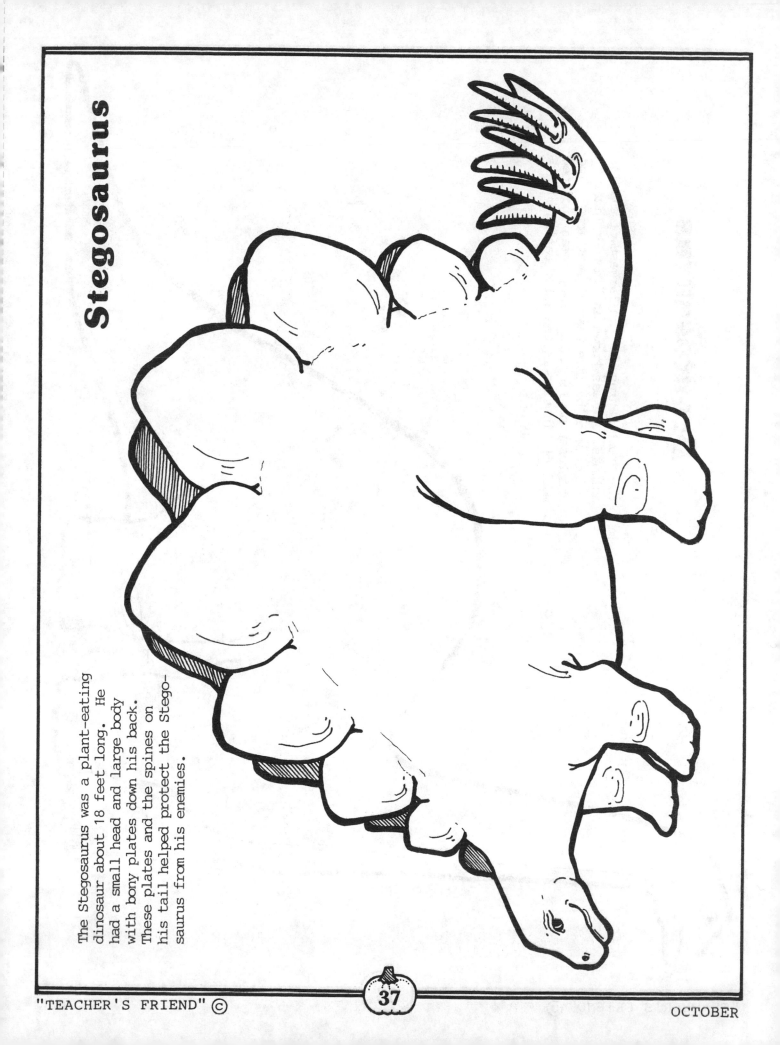

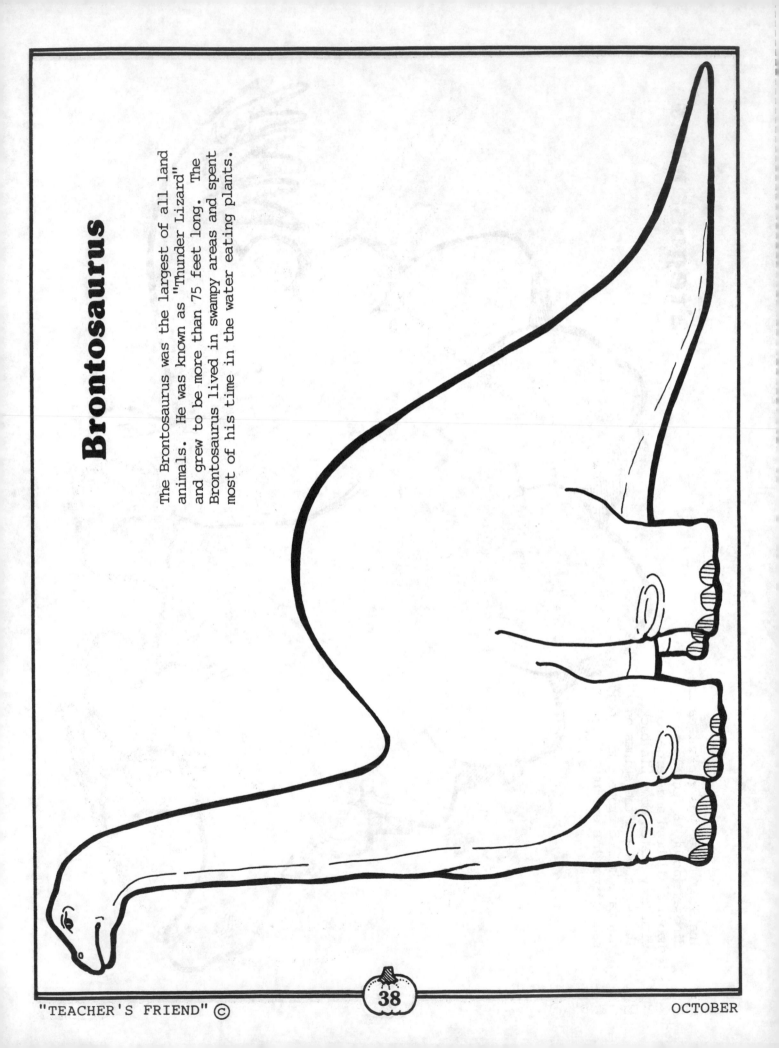

Brontosaurus

The Brontosaurus was the largest of all land animals. He was known as "Thunder Lizard" and grew to be more than 75 feet long. The Brontosaurus lived in swampy areas and spent most of his time in the water eating plants.

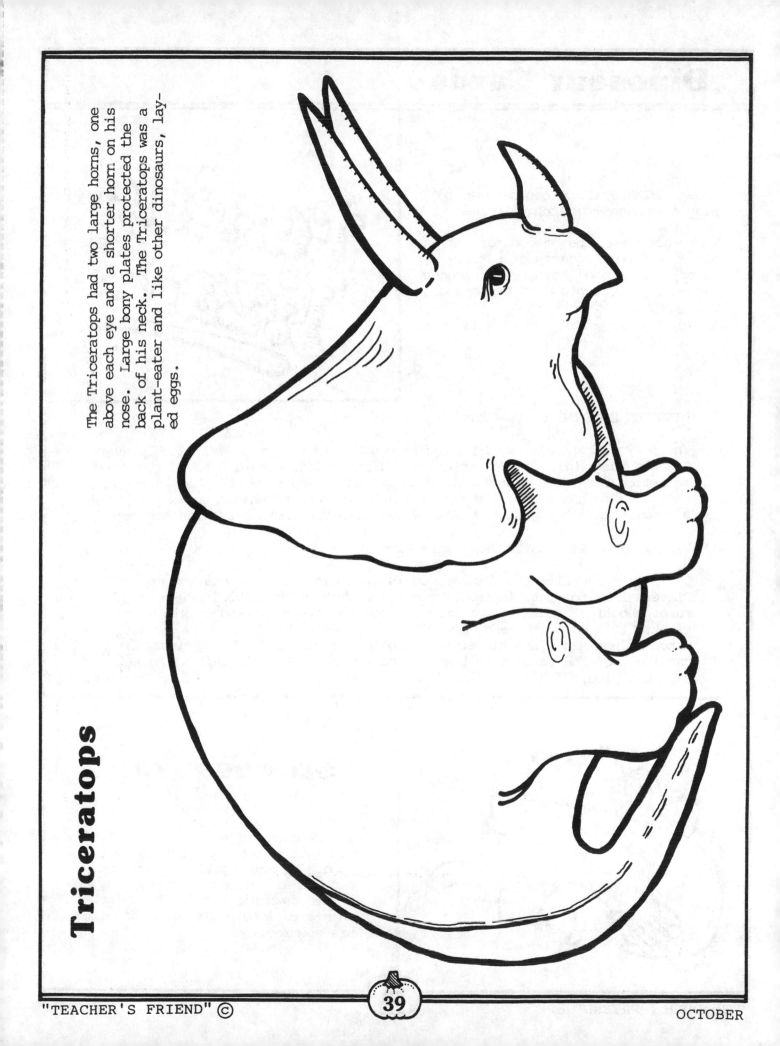

Triceratops

The Triceratops had two large horns, one above each eye and a shorter horn on his nose. Large bony plates protected the back of his neck. The Triceratops was a plant-eater and like other dinosaurs, layed eggs.

Dinosaur Cards

These DINOSAUR CARDS can be used to play a variety of matching games.

Reproduce the cards onto cardstock or paste them onto squares of poster-board. Color and laminate for longer durability. Let students try one of the games below.

DINOSAUR CONCENTRATION - Two Players

The players turn all of the cards face down, in random order. Each player takes a turn turning over two cards. If the picture card matches the description card, the player keeps the two cards and takes another turn. If the cards do not match, the player loses his turn to the other player. When all pairs have been matched, the player with the most pairs wins the game.

"TERRIBLE LIZARD" MATCH-UP - Three Players

One player shuffles the deck and deals five cards to each playing member. Players look for matching pairs and place them on the table. Players take turns choosing a card, sight unseen, from the player's hand on his or her right. If a match is made, the player lays down the matching pair. If a match is not made, the player holds on to the new card. The game continues until all of the cards have been paired and one player is left with the card entitled, "TERRIBLE LIZARD!"

Stegosaurus

The Stegosaurus was a medium sized dinosaur measuring about 18 feet long. He was a plant-eater that had a small head and large, bony plates down his back. The spines on his tail helped protect him from his enemies.

Dinosaur Cards

Triceratops

The Triceratops was a plant-eater that had to protect himself from many enemies. He had a large bony plate that covered the back of his neck and three long horns, one over each eye and another horn on his nose.

Pterodactyl

The Pterodactyl was a large flying reptile. He did not have feathers but rather horny scales. The wings were thin membranes, similar to the wings of a bat. The wing span of the Pterodactyl measured more than 20 feet.

Ankylosaurus

The Ankylosaurus was a plant-eater that was very well protected from his enemies. His body was almost completely covered with a hard, bony armor. He had long, sharp spikes down his sides and a powerful club-like tail.

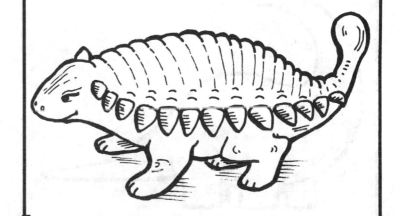

OCTOBER

Dinosaur Cards

Tyrannosaurus

The "King" of dinosaurs was the Tyrannosaurus. This giant meat-eater measured 45 feet when walking on his two back legs. He also had large, strong jaws and many sharp teeth.

Anatosaurus

The Anatosaurus was a large plant-eating dinosaur. He had a long, wide mouth that resembled a duck bill. These dinosaurs lived near or in the water where their webbed feet made them good swimmers.

Brontosaurus

The giant Brontosaurus was called "Thunder Lizard," apparently because the ground shook as he walked. This plant eater grew to be 75 feet long and spent most of his time in the water.

OCTOBER

Creative Writing

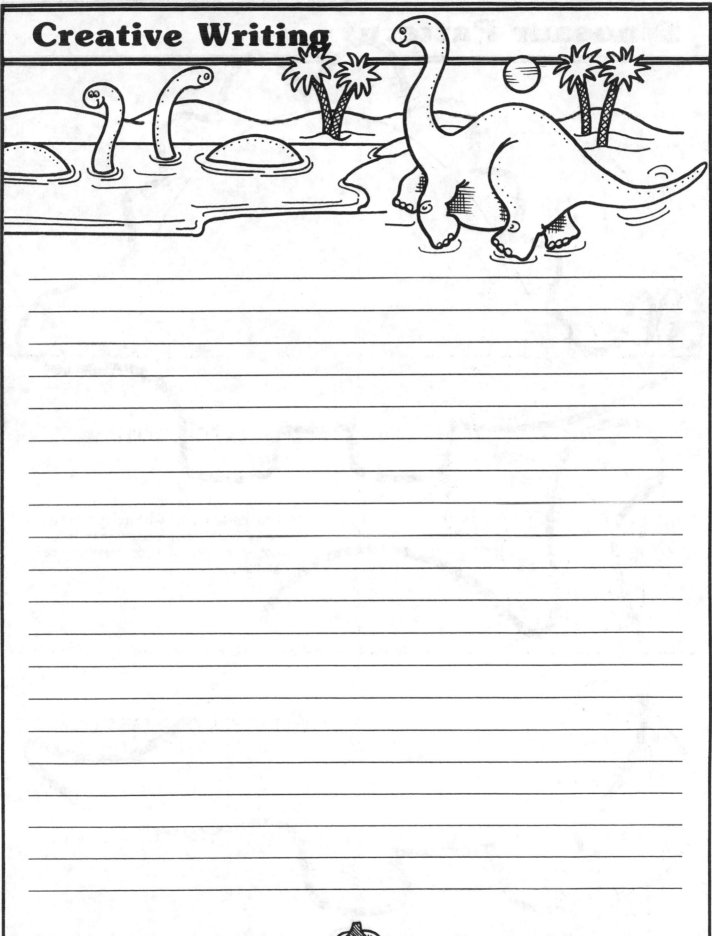

Dinosaur Patterns

Use these dinosaur patterns as name tags, calendar symbols, notes to parents or awards for students.

Masks

Masks Around the World

Throughout the history of the world, masks have played an important role in celebrations, death ceremonies and theatrical plays. Masks can cover the entire face or only part of the face. They can be made of a variety of materials, everything from wood, to paper, to gold.

Masks are very important in all African ceremonies. An African dancer might wear a beautiful mask of a spirit or animal. Masks are often believed to contain great powers and are handled with respect. Members of the tribe believe that a man can stop being himself, for a short time, when he disguises himself in a mask and costume.

Children might like to make an animal paper-bag mask. Older students could research the African cultures and find pictures of various ceremonial masks.

The Indian tribes of North America use masks in many ceremonies and rituals. The Iroquois people carve masks from living trees, which keep the masks "alive" and save their magical powers. The masks are painted red if cut in the morning and black, if cut later in the day. These "false faces" are carefully carved with the eyes rimmed with metal that glow in the light of the campfire. Horse tail hair is used in making wigs.

Have children draw pictures of masks that they think Iroquois warriors might make. Tell them to color the masks with bright colors and write brief descriptions about their masks.

OCTOBER

Masks Around the World

The Egyptians made death masks by making wax impressions of the deceased face. These masks were covered with sheets of gold and were believed to protect the deceased from evil spirits.

Show the class pictures of King Tutankhamen's treasures including his death mask. Students might like to make life-size sculptures of their own faces from clay. Later, paper mache masks can be made over the face sculptures. When dry, they can spray paint the masks gold and display them on a bulletin board entitled "Our Egyptian Masks."

The ancient people of Mexico and South America made beautiful relief masks of thin sheets of gold. These early craftsmen used gold for their designs because it was easy to work with and so very plentiful. These masks were usually used to tell stories and for entertainment.

Buy several sheets of copper or brass foil from local craft stores. (Heavy-duty aluminum foil can also work well.) Using dull pencils to draw designs, students can simulate the artwork done by Latin craftsmen.

Early Greeks wore animal masks to worship their gods. Later, this developed into theatrical use where actors wore masks on stage. One man could play several roles by simply changing masks. The masks often contained small megaphones to help the actor be heard. Greek theatrical masks usually fell into two categories, tragedy or comedy.

Have students act out short skits using masks. They might like to create original plays or use familiar stories, such as, fairy tales or nursery rhymes.

OCTOBER

Masks Around the World

Eskimos of Alaska carve ceremonial masks from driftwood that is washed in by the sea. The men of the tribe often make these masks to represent spirits that give them good luck in fishing and hunting. Eagle feathers, seal skin and animal fur are usually used as decoration. The masks are worn during ceremonial dances.

The Eskimo women carve small masks that fit easily on their fingers. During the dance, they wave their hands and finger masks to the rhythm of the music. Every Eskimo dance tells a story. The dancer often makes up the story as the dance continues.

Eskimo Finger Mask

Make this Eskimo Finger Mask from construction paper. Cut out and color as you wish. Cut holes for your fingers. Fringe may be cut along the outside edge.

OCTOBER

Creative Writing

OCTOBER

Mask Patterns

Cut the mask and patterns from construction paper and have children create a variety of different masks for any costume.

Children will love using their imaginations to create faces and characters. Let them add pipe cleaner whiskers, glitter, cotton and sequins for that extra special look.

CAT AND BUNNY NOSE

CAT EARS

OWL FEATHERS

HORNS

BEAK

EYE LIDS

PIGGY EARS

PIGGY NOSE

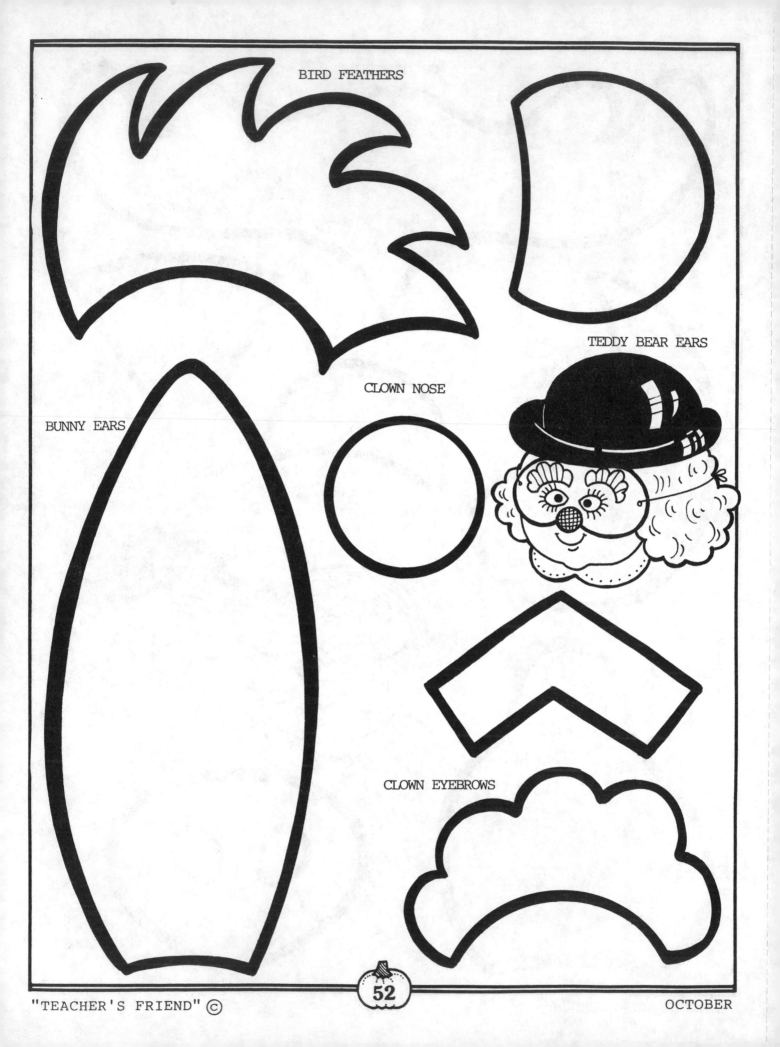

BIRD FEATHERS

TEDDY BEAR EARS

CLOWN NOSE

BUNNY EARS

CLOWN EYEBROWS

OCTOBER

GLAMOR EYES

DOG EARS

NOSE AND MUSTACHE

DOG OR TEDDY BEAR NOSE

Happy Mask

The Happy and Sad Masks can be used in role-playing activities with your students.

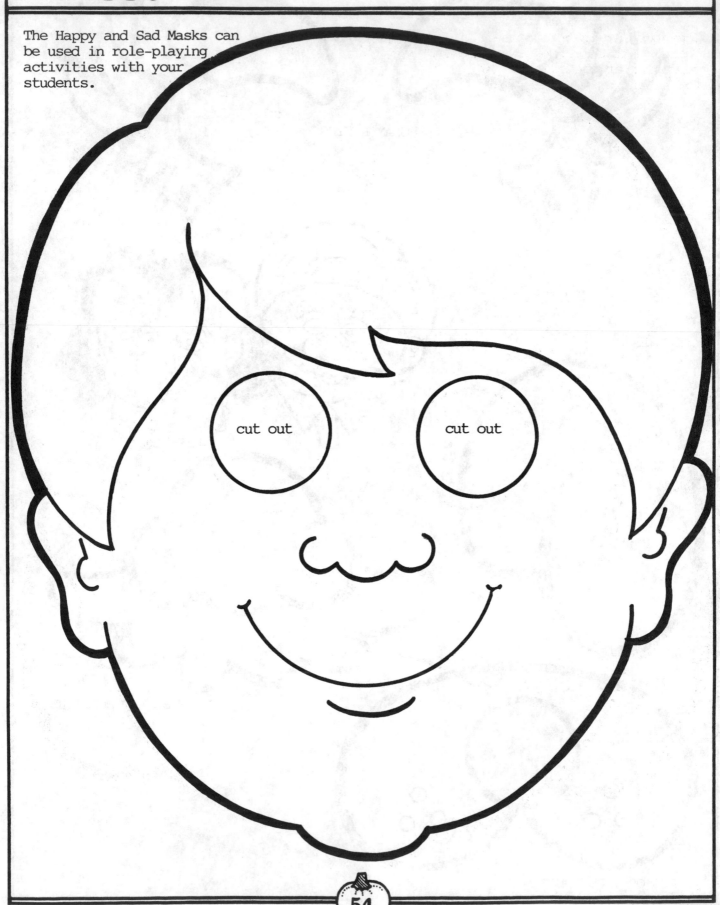

cut out

cut out

Sad Mask

Copy both masks onto poster board. Attach a tongue depressor at the chin for a handle.

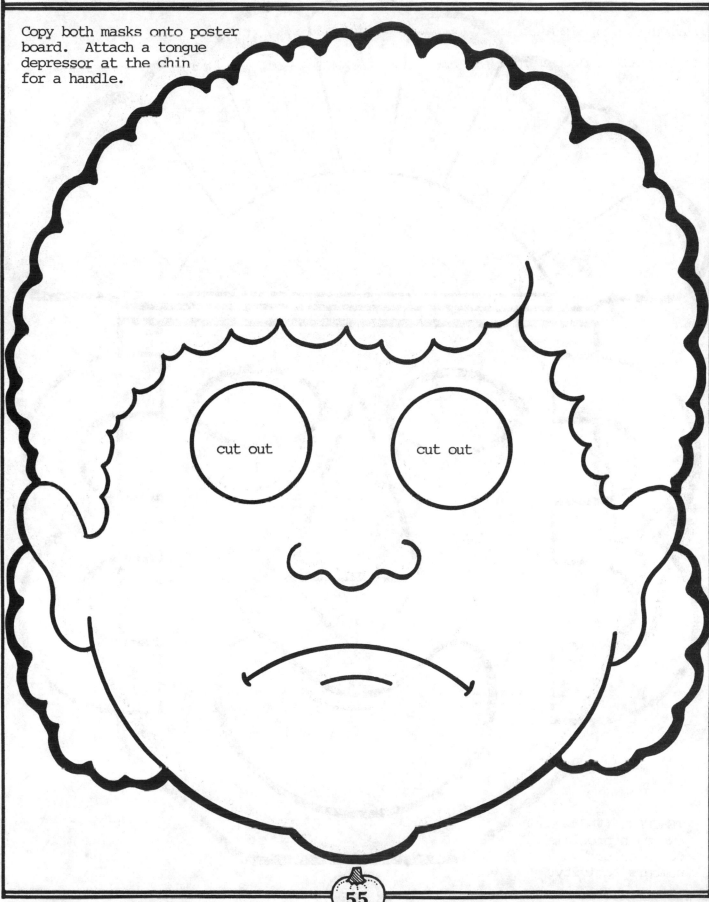

cut out

cut out

TEACHERS: Add your own math problems for a color by numbers activity.

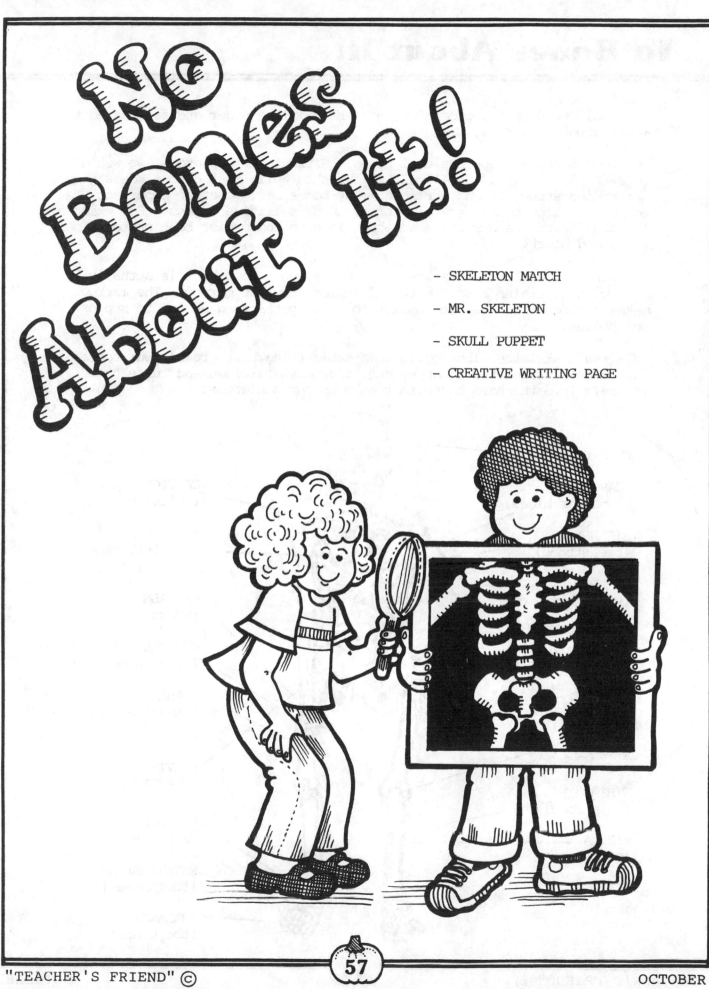

No Bones About It!

- SKELETON MATCH

- MR. SKELETON

- SKULL PUPPET

- CREATIVE WRITING PAGE

No Bones About It!

With Halloween fast approaching, students will be eager and fascinated to learn about skeletons.

Our bodies contain 206 skeletal bones. Without our skeletons, we would be a shapeless mass, much like a jellyfish. While most of our bones give our bodies structure and strength, many bones serve another important purpose. These bones carefully protect our sensitive organs. For example, the skull protects our brain and our rib cage and breast bone protects our lungs and heart.

The bones in our skeletons are very much alive. Each bone is actually hollow and contains a soft material inside known as marrow. The marrow makes our bones lighter and easier to move, yet strong enough to support our bodies.

This rigid skeleton also does a remarkable thing. It grows! Our bodies take minerals from the foods we eat, one being calcium, and turns these minerals into the hard bones that make up our skeletons.

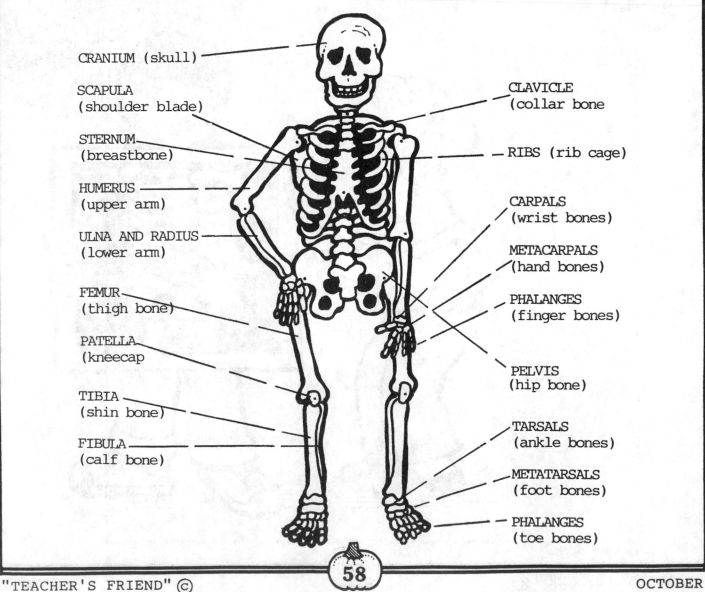

CRANIUM (skull)

SCAPULA
(shoulder blade)

STERNUM
(breastbone)

HUMERUS
(upper arm)

ULNA AND RADIUS
(lower arm)

FEMUR
(thigh bone)

PATELLA
(kneecap

TIBIA
(shin bone)

FIBULA
(calf bone)

CLAVICLE
(collar bone

RIBS (rib cage)

CARPALS
(wrist bones)

METACARPALS
(hand bones)

PHALANGES
(finger bones)

PELVIS
(hip bone)

TARSALS
(ankle bones)

METATARSALS
(foot bones)

PHALANGES
(toe bones)

OCTOBER

Skeleton Match

After your students have become familiar with the common and proper names for the major bones, play a "Simple Simon" type of game. "Mr. Skeleton says......touch your cranium."

ACTIVITY 2

MATCH THE COMMON NAMES OF BONES WITH THEIR PROPER NAMES.

CRANIUM	Collar Bone
FIBULA	Kneecap
PATELLA	Hand and Foot Bones
ULNA AND RADIUS	Shoulder Blade
SCAPULA	Calf Bone
STERNUM	Thigh Bone
HUMERUS	Breastbone
FEMUR	Shin Bone
TIBIA	Finger and Toe Bones
CLAVICLE	Hip Bone
PELVIS	Ankle Bones
METACARPALS/METATARSALS	Skull
PHALANGES	Wrist Bones
CARPALS	Upper Arm Bone
TARSALS	Lower Arm Bones

OCTOBER

Mr. Skeleton

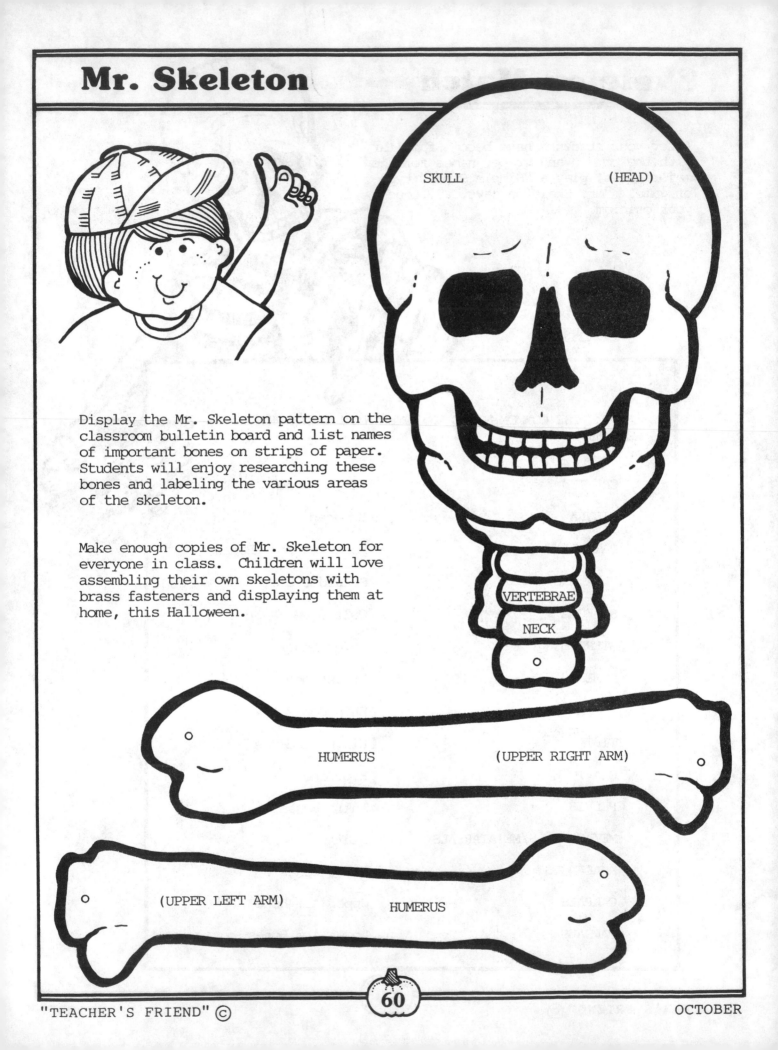

Display the Mr. Skeleton pattern on the classroom bulletin board and list names of important bones on strips of paper. Students will enjoy researching these bones and labeling the various areas of the skeleton.

Make enough copies of Mr. Skeleton for everyone in class. Children will love assembling their own skeletons with brass fasteners and displaying them at home, this Halloween.

SKULL   (HEAD)

VERTEBRAE

NECK

HUMERUS   (UPPER RIGHT ARM)

(UPPER LEFT ARM)   HUMERUS

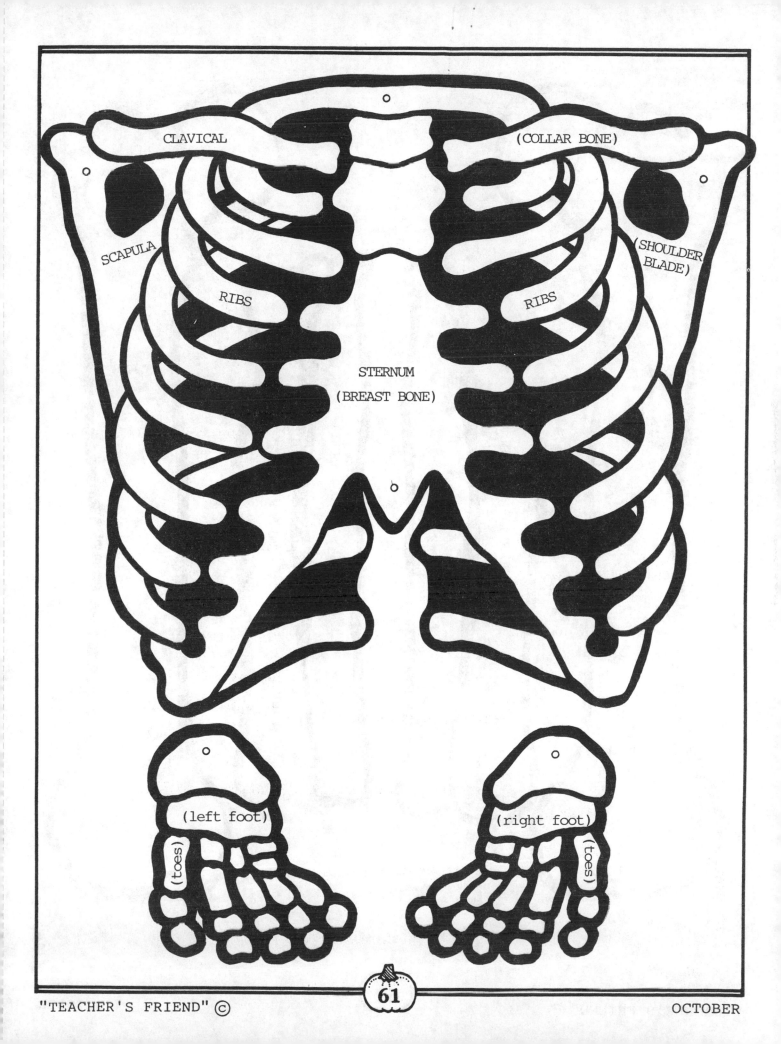

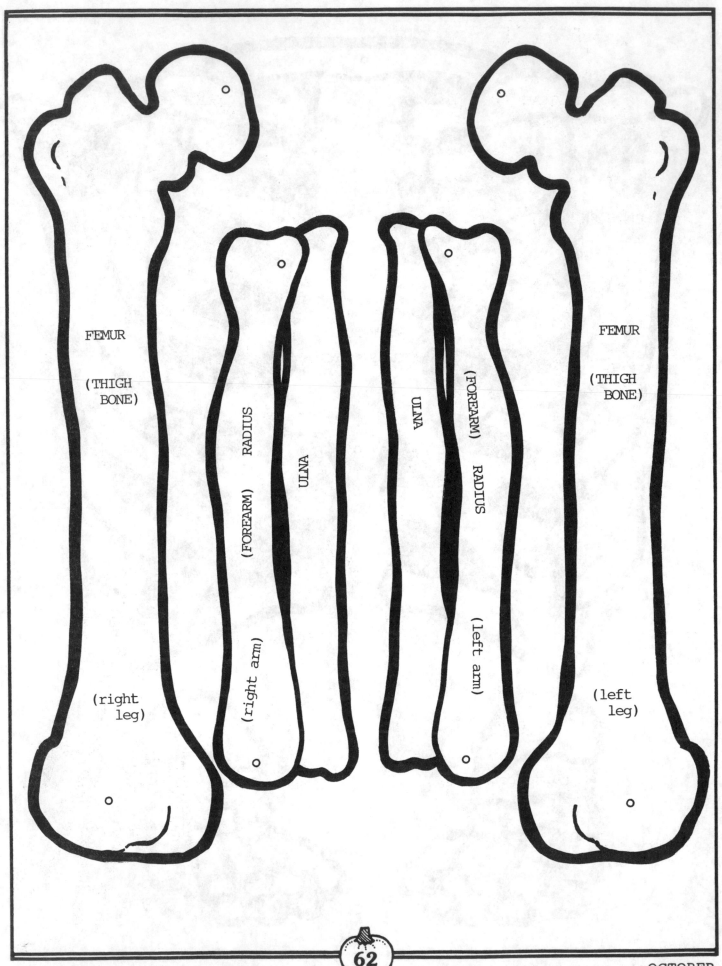

FEMUR

(THIGH BONE)

RADIUS (FOREARM)

ULNA

ULNA

(FOREARM) RADIUS

FEMUR

(THIGH BONE)

(right leg)

(right arm)

(left arm)

(left leg)

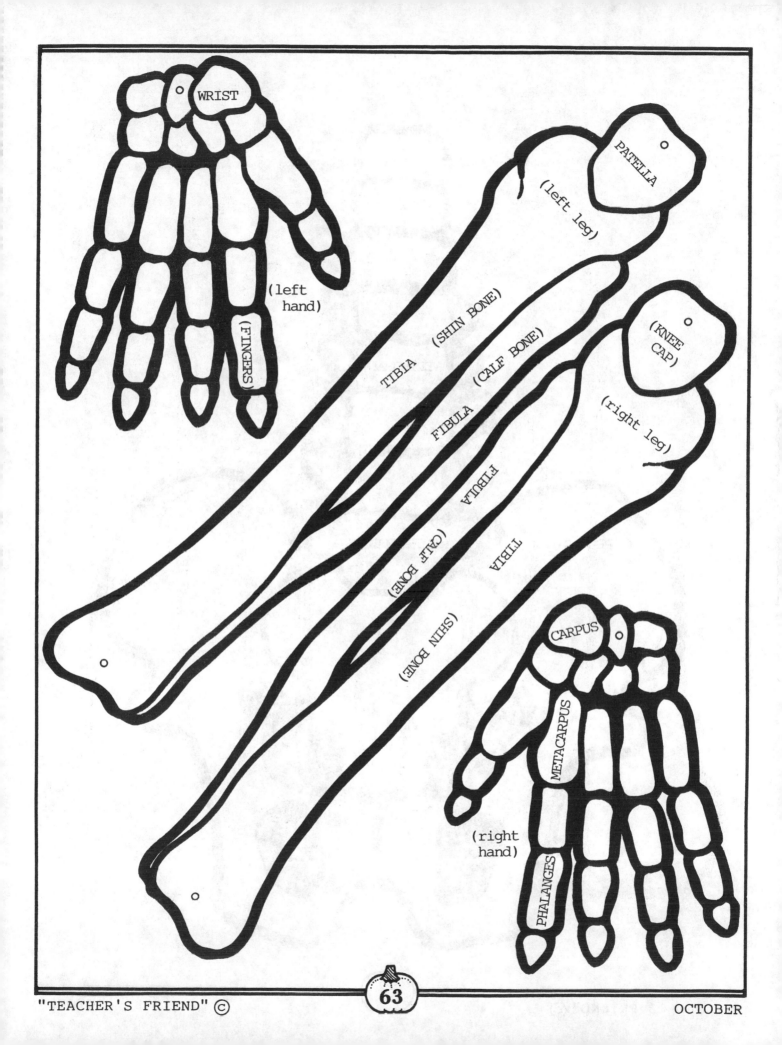

WRIST

(left
hand)

(FINGERS)

PATELLA

(left leg)

TIBIA (SHIN BONE)

FIBULA (CALF BONE)

(KNEE
CAP)

(right leg)

FIBULA (CALF BONE)

TIBIA (SHIN BONE)

CARPUS

METACARPUS

PHALANGES

(right
hand)

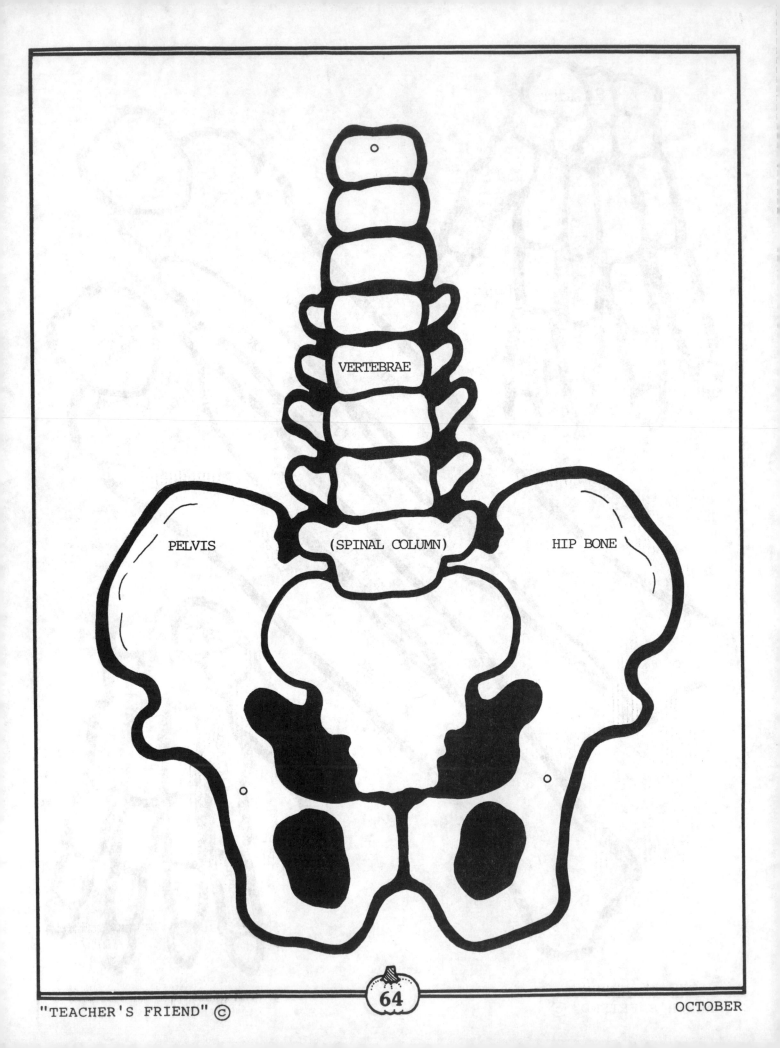

VERTEBRAE

PELVIS   (SPINAL COLUMN)   HIP BONE

OCTOBER

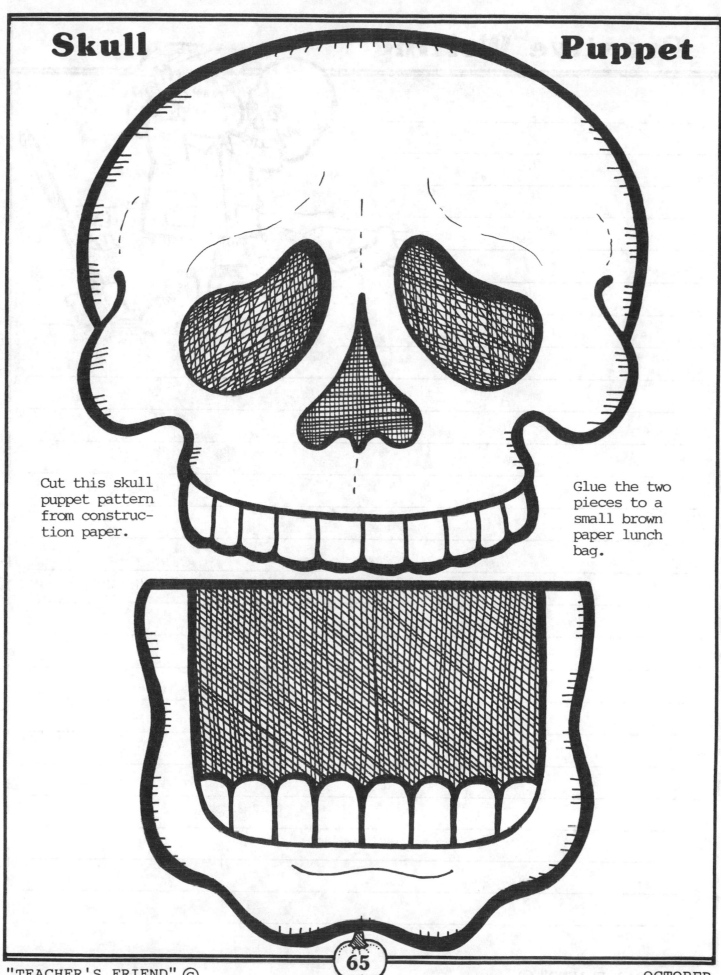

Skull Puppet

Cut this skull puppet pattern from construction paper.

Glue the two pieces to a small brown paper lunch bag.

"TEACHER'S FRIEND" ©

OCTOBER

Creative Writing

_____

_____

_____

_____

_____

_____

_____

_____

_____

_____

_____

_____

_____

_____

_____

_____

_____

_____

_____

_____

OCTOBER

- CHRISTOPHER COLUMBUS

- DISCOVERY MAP

- NIÑA, PINTA AND SANTA MARIA

- COLOR PAGE

- CREATIVE WRITING PAGE

- SHIP PATTERN

October 12th

Christopher Columbus

On August 3, 1492, Christopher Columbus set sail from Spain in search of the East Indies. Columbus sailed west across the uncharted Atlantic Ocean. Eighty-eight men made up the crews of the "Niña," "Pinta" and "Santa Maria."

The journey was a long and difficult one. The crews became terrified at their failure to find land and made threats of mutiny. Before dawn, on October 12, 1492, the ships landed on an island in the Bahamas. With island natives looking on, Columbus reverently claimed the land for Spain and called it "San Salvador." He was disappointed not to find the wealthy cities and grand civilizations that had been speculated. Instead he found a primitive world where shy people still lived in grass huts.

Columbus had discovered the New World, however, and for this he was honored by King Ferdinand and Queen Isabella of Spain. The land Columbus discovered soon became known as "America," after Amerigo Vespucci, who later explored the mainland for Portugal. One thing is for sure, Christopher Columbus was a man of vision and courage. He conquered the Atlantic Ocean and opened the New World for others to follow.

ACTIVITY 3

FIND THESE WORDS IN THE PUZZLE BELOW: COLUMBUS, NIÑA, PINTA, SANTA MARIA, SPAIN, SAN SALVADOR, NEW WORLD, AMERICA, KING FERDINAND, QUEEN ISABELLA

```
D V B H Y U J K O L M N H G V B H F R T Y
C O L U M B U S S E R T G Y H U J K I L P
W E R T G Y H P D C V B Q S E R T Y U I P
Z C V F G T H A S W R T U F G H Y U J M N
C F G R T B N I F R T Y E D R Y H J P S Q
S C V B G F D N R T Y H E C O L K I I N G
A M E T Y F E B C D R W N Q X C V T N H U
N E S A N T A M A R I A I F V B G T T D R
S W E T Y G H U I J K Y S D R T Y E A V F
B G T Y U J H F G T V B A M E R I C A T U
W E R T G D V F H F T R B W T Y U P I B N
Q U E F T G H K I N G F E R D I N A N D R
D C V G H B G F V F D S L S R T G Y T R E
D N E W W O R L D F T E L F R T Y G F R E
F B V C D S A N S A L V A D O R F T Y H U
S D F G T Y H U J N B V C X Z D R T G D R
S R V B N M K J G F D N I Ñ A S E F Y H O
```

OCTOBER

Discovery Map

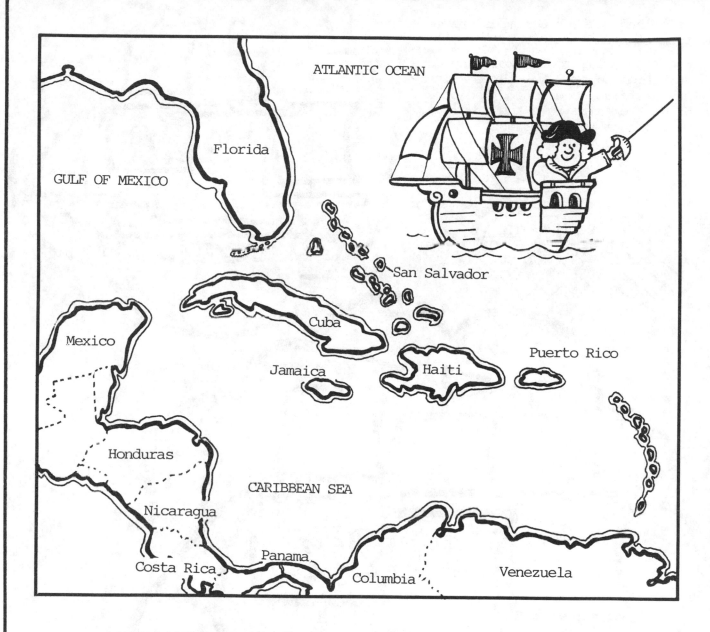

The discovery made by Christopher Columbus changed the history of the world. Write a story using one of these ideas:

You are Christopher Columbus and about to set sail for the New World.

You are a crew member of the "Santa Maria."

You are a native that has just seen three strange ships approaching your island.

You are Isabella I, Queen of Spain.

Niña, Pinta and.....

Color and cut out Columbus' three ships from construction paper.

Fan-fold a large sheet of blue construction paper. Cut three slits in the folds, one behind the other. Slide the ships into the openings making them stand upright.

This clever craft will make a wonderful display for Columbus Day.

Color Page

TEACHERS: Add your own math problems.

Columbus

Creative Writing

OCTOBER

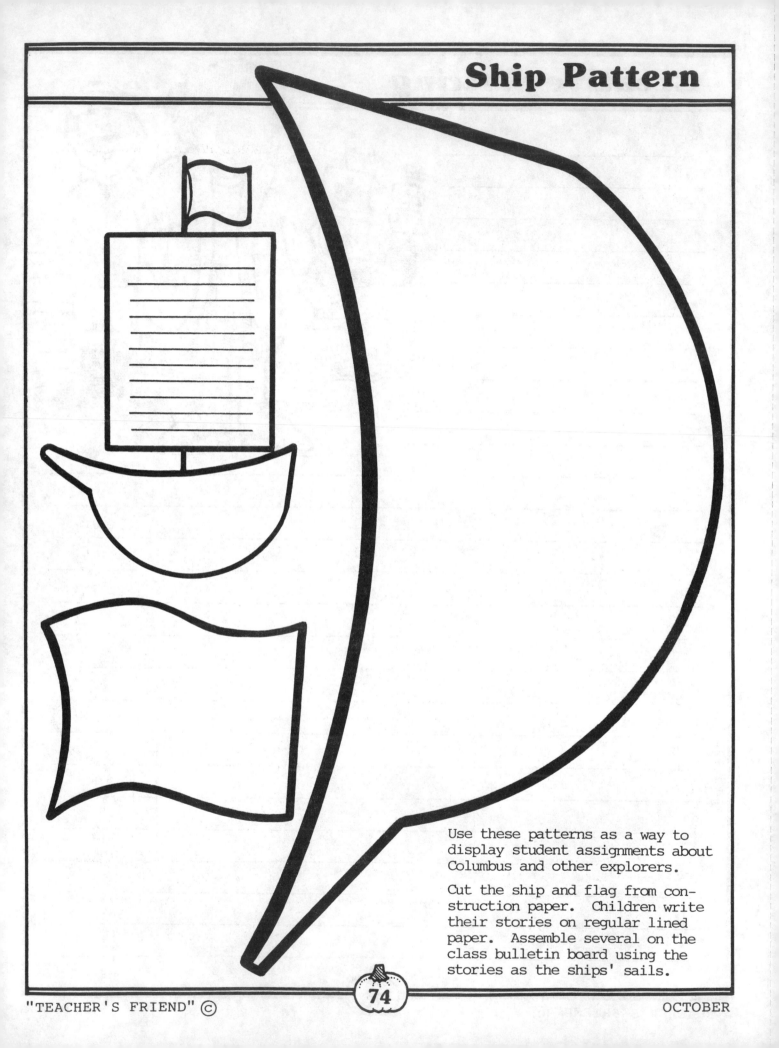

Use these patterns as a way to display student assignments about Columbus and other explorers.

Cut the ship and flag from construction paper. Children write their stories on regular lined paper. Assemble several on the class bulletin board using the stories as the ships' sails.

- FIRE SAFETY ACTIVITIES
- FIREMAN'S HAT AND CERTIFICATE
- MY FIRE SAFETY BOOK
- FIRE SAFETY QUESTIONNAIRE

Fire Prevention Day
October 9th

OCTOBER

Fire Safety Activities

1. Ask students to find newspaper accounts of recent fires. Read them to the class and conduct discussions as to how they could have been prevented.

2. Suggest that students question friends and family members to learn what experiences they have had with fire. Have the children tell the class their findings and let the students participate in deciding what should have been done in the same circumstances.

3. Ask students to research fire safety pertaining to a particular holiday. Students might like to choose the 4th of July, with it's fireworks, Christmas, with it's lights and candles or Halloween, with it's jack-o'-lanterns.

4. On the chalk board, draw a map of your class's fire drill route. Tell the children about the importance of following the rules and the need to be speedy during a fire emergency.

5. Instruct students on what to do if their clothing catches fire. Select one child to demonstrate to the class how to roll on the floor. Another child can pretend to smother the flames with a blanket. Ask students to discuss how this type of fire emergency could be prevented.

6. Arrange for a firefighter to visit your class. Before his or her visit, have students list questions that they wish to ask.

7. Have students role-play an emergency in which a neighbor's house is burning. Students can use a toy telephone to practice dialing the emergency number and giving the information needed by the fire department.

Create an informative bulletin board by enlarging a large telephone onto poster board. Emergency numbers should be listed for children's information.

Students might like to find pictures of possible fire dangers and display them on the board with various fire safety guidelines.

Fireman's Hat

Enlarge this simple pattern onto 12" X 18" red construction paper. Cut out where indicated and fold back. Students can glue a yellow "Jr. Fire Dept." badge to the center. Children will love to wear their new hats home.

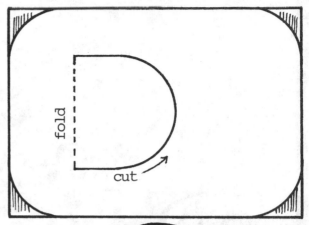

Fire Safety Certificate

_____

has promised to be fire safety conscious and to follow fire safety rules

_____   _____

OCTOBER

My Fire Safety Book

Name _____

PLAN ESCAPE ROUTES WITH YOUR FAMILY.
DRAW A PICTURE OF THE FLOOR PLAN OF
YOUR HOUSE AND INDICATE THE ROUTES
FAMILY MEMBERS WILL TAKE.

PARENT'S SIGNATURE _____

STUDENT'S SIGNATURE _____

OCTOBER

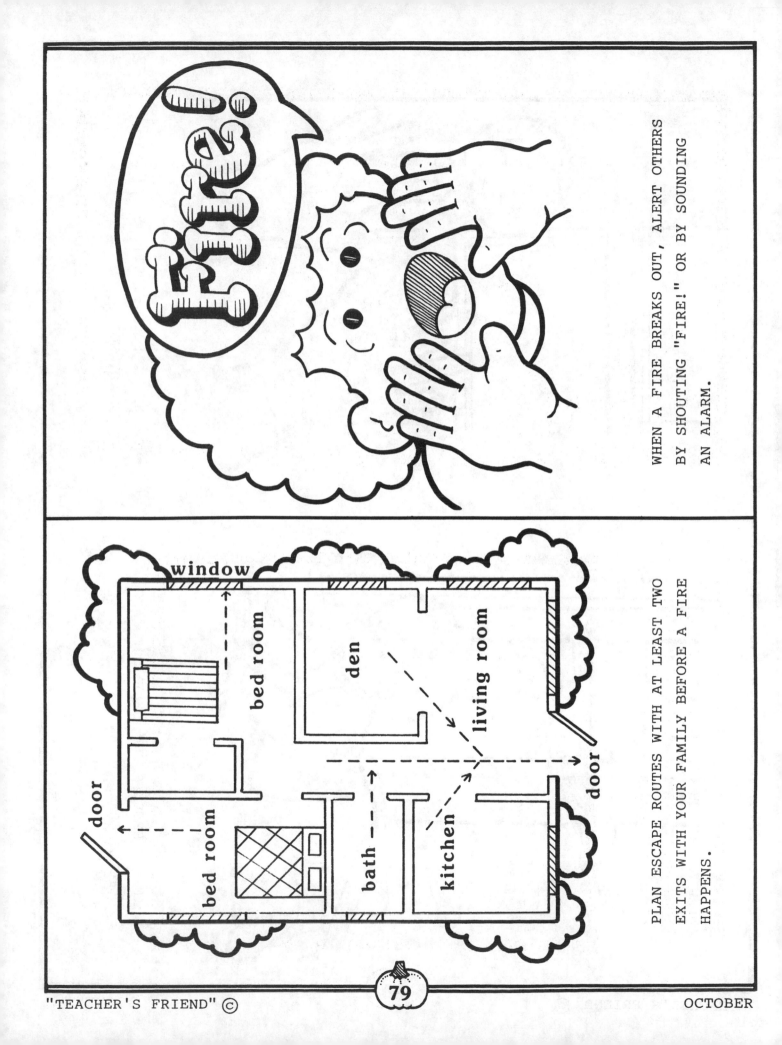

WHEN A FIRE BREAKS OUT, ALERT OTHERS BY SHOUTING "FIRE!" OR BY SOUNDING AN ALARM.

PLAN ESCAPE ROUTES WITH AT LEAST TWO EXITS WITH YOUR FAMILY BEFORE A FIRE HAPPENS.

OCTOBER

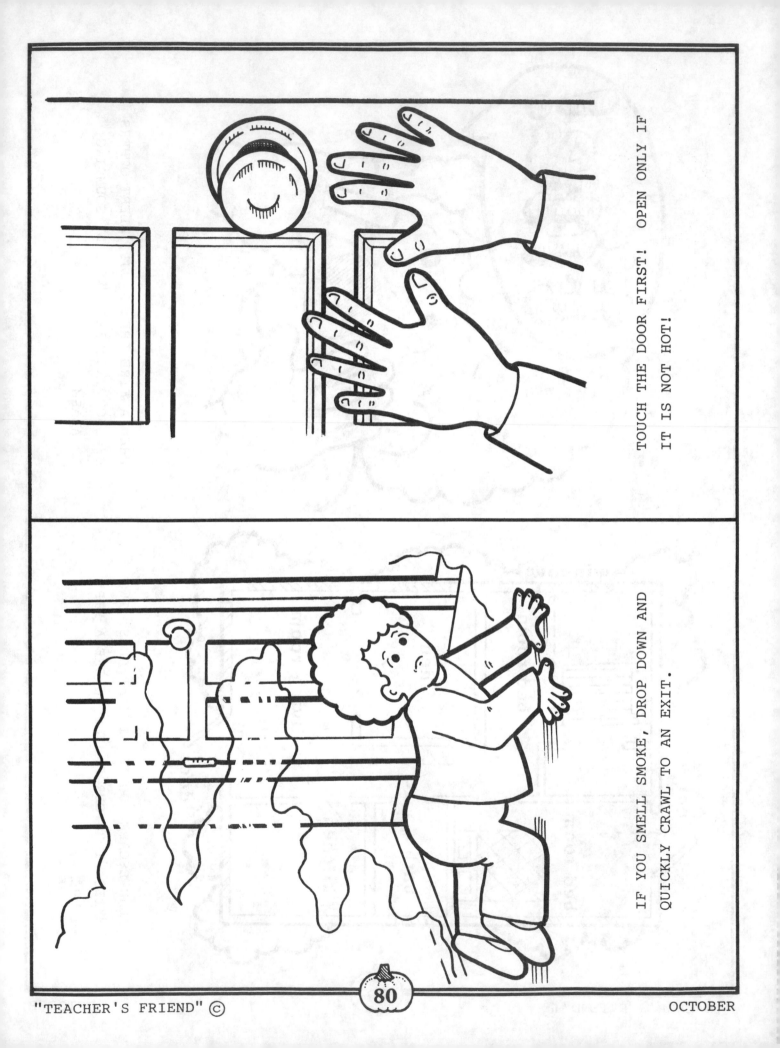

TOUCH THE DOOR FIRST! OPEN ONLY IF IT IS NOT HOT!

IF YOU SMELL SMOKE, DROP DOWN AND QUICKLY CRAWL TO AN EXIT.

EMERGENCY
PHONE
NUMBER

CALL THE FIRE DEPARTMENT FROM A
NEIGHBOR'S HOUSE.

ONCE YOU ARE OUTSIDE,
STAY OUT!

FOLLOW YOUR BEST ESCAPE ROUTE AS
QUICKLY AS POSSIBLE. MEET OTHER
FAMILY MEMBERS OUTDOORS.

OCTOBER

Fire Safety Questionnaire

YES	NO	Do you know the emergency number to call in case of fire?
YES	NO	Have you planned a fire escape route with your family? Does each family member know what to do?
YES	NO	Do you know how to roll on the floor in case your clothing catches fire?
YES	NO	Does your family have at least one fire extinguisher? Does everyone in the family know where it is and how to use it?
YES	NO	Are all lamp and appliance cords in good shape?
YES	NO	Are there smoke detectors placed in the living and bedroom areas of the house?
YES	NO	Are portable heaters kept away from drapes, furniture and other flammable materials?
YES	NO	Does the fireplace have a close-fitting screen or closure?
YES	NO	Do adults know not to smoke in bed?
YES	NO	Are cooking pot handles kept out of reach of small children?
YES	NO	Are curtains and towels kept away from the stove and open flames?
YES	NO	Are foods always supervised during cooking?
YES	NO	Is trash, paper and flammable liquids kept away from furnace and water heaters?
YES	NO	Is gasoline kept in a safe place and tightly capped?
YES	NO	Are oily rags cleaned up or stored in tightly sealed metal containers?
YES	NO	Are dried weeds, leaves and other trash kept away from the house and cleaned up quickly?
YES	NO	If your family barbecues, do they know how to safely light and extinguish charcoal?
YES	NO	Do family members know how to safely refuel a gasoline lawn mower?

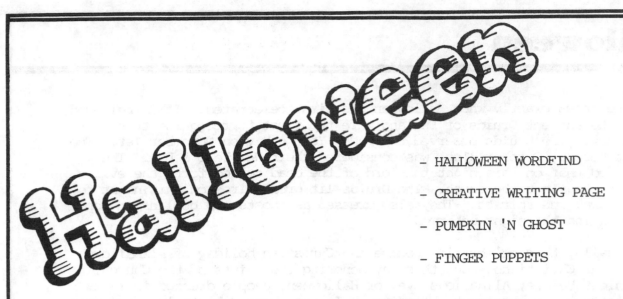

Halloween

October 31st

TRICK OR TREAT

OCTOBER

Halloween

No one knows exactly when Halloween was first celebrated. It is believed that the ancient Druids of England were the first to recognize this special day. The Druids observed their New Year's Day on November 1st. The night before, October 31st, was considered their New Year's Eve. They believed that on this night the lord of the dead called forth the evil spirits to visit the earth. The Druids lit great fires on this night to scare away the spirits. They also dressed as ghosts and goblins in hopes of escaping the night unharmed.

Eventually, this celebration became the Christian holiday of Allhallows Day. The Christians spent this day honoring the saints of the Church. The night before, Allhallows Eve, or Halloween, people dressed in masks and costumes to represent the saints. It was their duty to lead the spirits of the dead out of town before celebrations the next day.

After the Romans conquered Britain, harvest festivals became a part of the celebrations. In Scotland, people carried torches through the fields in hopes of a good crop for the next year. Lit torches were also carried to frighten away witches and ghosts that might be hiding in orchards and pastures. Potatoes and turnips were hollowed out and carved by people in Ireland. Lit candles were placed inside to scare evil spirits away.

Halloween has changed through the years. Next to Christmas, Halloween is the favorite holiday of many children. It is a time to dress up and pretend and explore the neighborhood searching for treats.

When writing spooky Halloween stories, have students try using some of these colorful words in place of the common words; witch, ghost, scary, and dark.

WITCH:

   hag
   sorceress
   soothsayer
   siren
   demon
   warlock

GHOST:

   ghoul
   phantom
   spirit
   spook
   fiend
   poltergeist

SCARY:

   frightful
   spooky
   awesome
   grim
   horrifying
   ghastly
   terrifying
   fiendish

DARK:

   vague
   cloudy
   hazy
   shadow
   foggy
   dim
   gloomy

Word Find

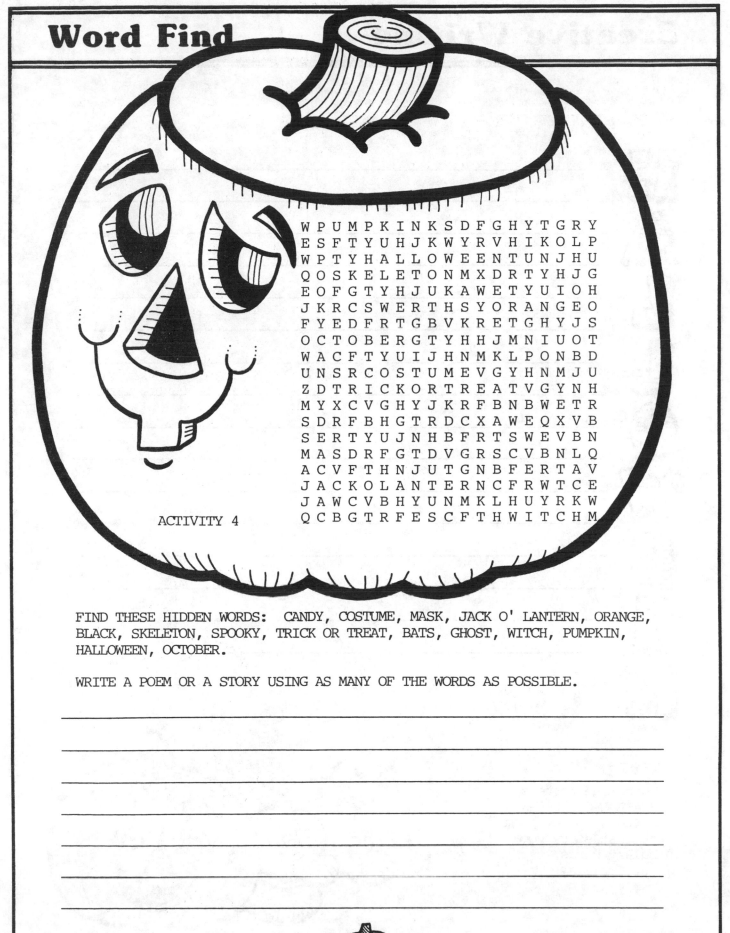

```
W P U M P K I N K S D F G H Y T G R Y
E S F T Y U H J K W Y R V H I K O L P
W P T Y H A L L O W E E N T U N J H U
Q O S K E L E T O N M X D R T Y H J G
E O F G T Y H J U K A W E T Y U I O H
J K R C S W E R T H S Y O R A N G E O
F Y E D F R T G B V K R E T G H Y J S
O C T O B E R G T Y H H J M N I U O T
W A C F T Y U I J H N M K L P O N B D
U N S R C O S T U M E V G Y H N M J U
Z D T R I C K O R T R E A T V G Y N W
M Y X C V G H Y J K R F B N B W E T R
S D R F B H G T R D C X A W E Q X V B
S E R T Y U J N H B F R T S W E V B N
M A S D R F G T D V G R S C V B N L Q
A C V F T H N J U T G N B F E R T A V
J A C K O L A N T E R N C F R W T C E
J A W C V B H Y U N M K L H U Y R K W
Q C B G T R F E S C F T H W I T C H M
```

ACTIVITY 4

FIND THESE HIDDEN WORDS: CANDY, COSTUME, MASK, JACK O' LANTERN, ORANGE, BLACK, SKELETON, SPOOKY, TRICK OR TREAT, BATS, GHOST, WITCH, PUMPKIN, HALLOWEEN, OCTOBER.

WRITE A POEM OR A STORY USING AS MANY OF THE WORDS AS POSSIBLE.

_____

_____

_____

_____

_____

_____

OCTOBER

Creative Writing

HALLOWEEN

_____
_____
_____
_____
_____
_____
_____
_____
_____
_____
_____
_____
_____
_____
_____
_____
_____

Using the letters
H-A-L-L-O-W-E-E-N,
write a spooky poem
or list scary voca-
bulary words.

OCTOBER

Pumpkin 'n Ghost

Cut the two pumpkin pieces and the ghost from construction paper. Assemble with a brass fastener.

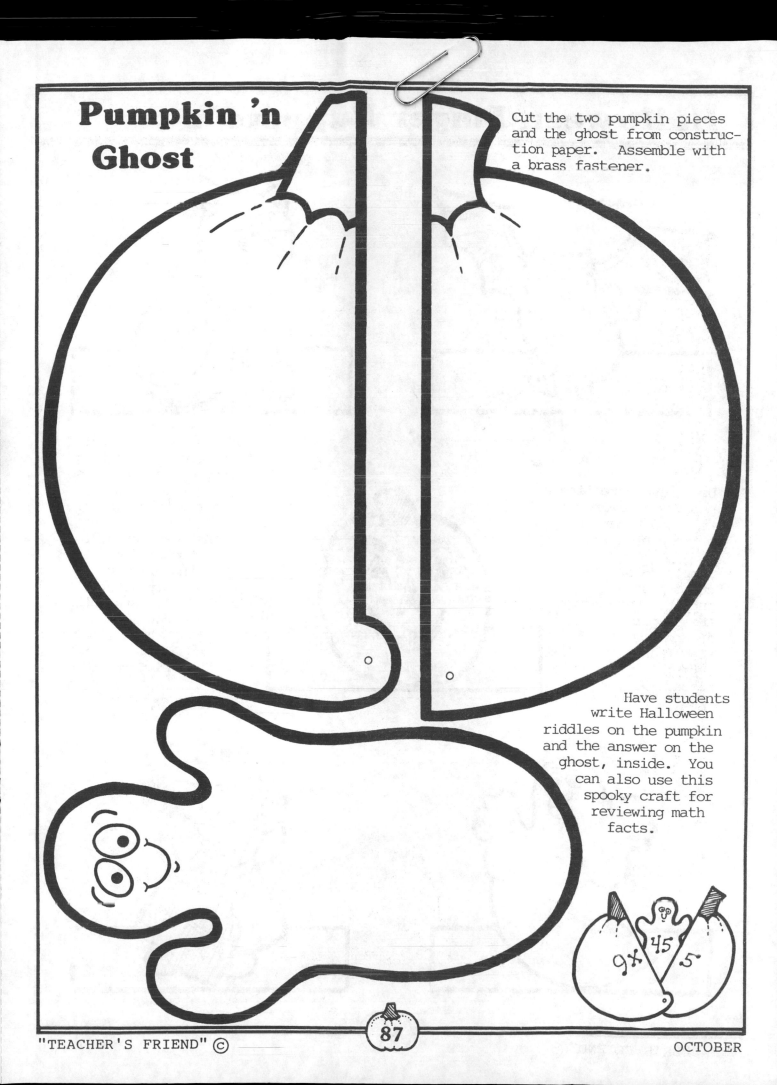

Have students write Halloween riddles on the pumpkin and the answer on the ghost, inside. You can also use this spooky craft for reviewing math facts.

9X 45 5

Halloween Finger Puppets

Students will be eager to do creative writing assignments with these finger puppets as motivators.

Use these cute finger puppets as awards for good behavior or completed work.

Simply color and cut out each puppet. Bend the puppet around your finger and tape in place.

Ask each child to choose a puppet and write a story about it. Students can act out their stories in front of the class.

OCTOBER

Matching Ghosts

Make several ghosts
from white construc-
tion paper. Cut each
ghost in half. Label
each half with a matching
word or problem.

You might like
to try matching
homonyms, oppo-
site words, Roman
numerals, upper
and lower case
letters or frac-
tions.

Students solve the prob-
lems and match the
ghost halves together.

Help the Witch Find Her Broom!

Assemble both pages on poster board for a cute Halloween gameboard.

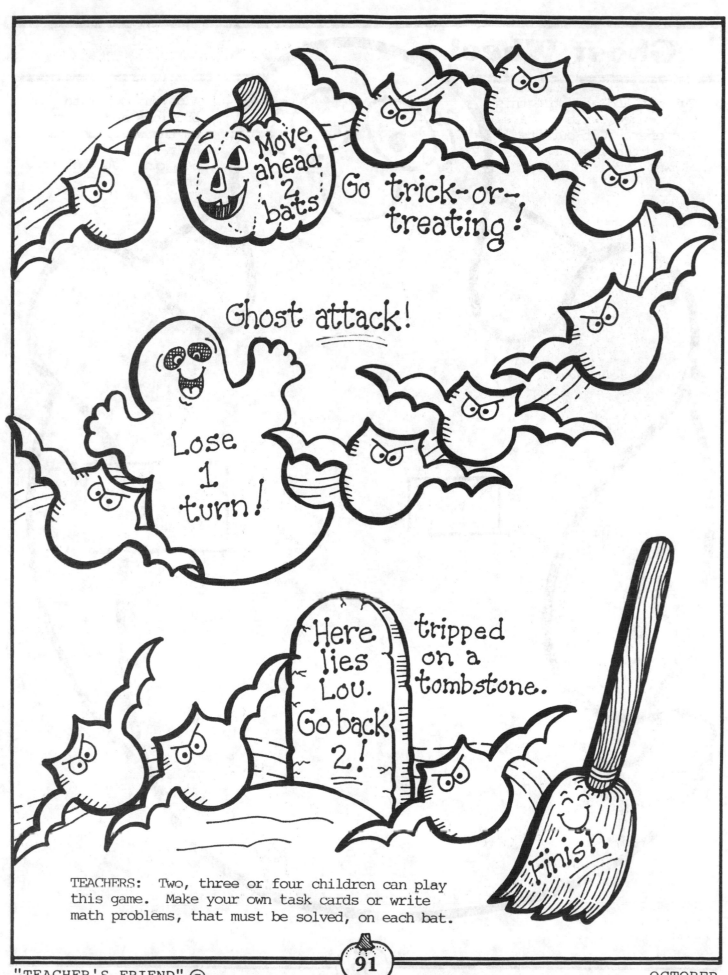

Move ahead 2 bats

Go trick-or-treating!

Ghost attack!

Lose 1 turn!

Here lies Lou. Go back 2!

tripped on a tombstone.

Finish

TEACHERS: Two, three or four children can play this game. Make your own task cards or write math problems, that must be solved, on each bat.

Ghost Wheel

Cut out and assemble this Ghost Wheel with a brass fastener. Cut out the two rectangles, as shown.

Add your own math problems and answers to the wheel on the next page. Move the pumpkin to reveal the answer.

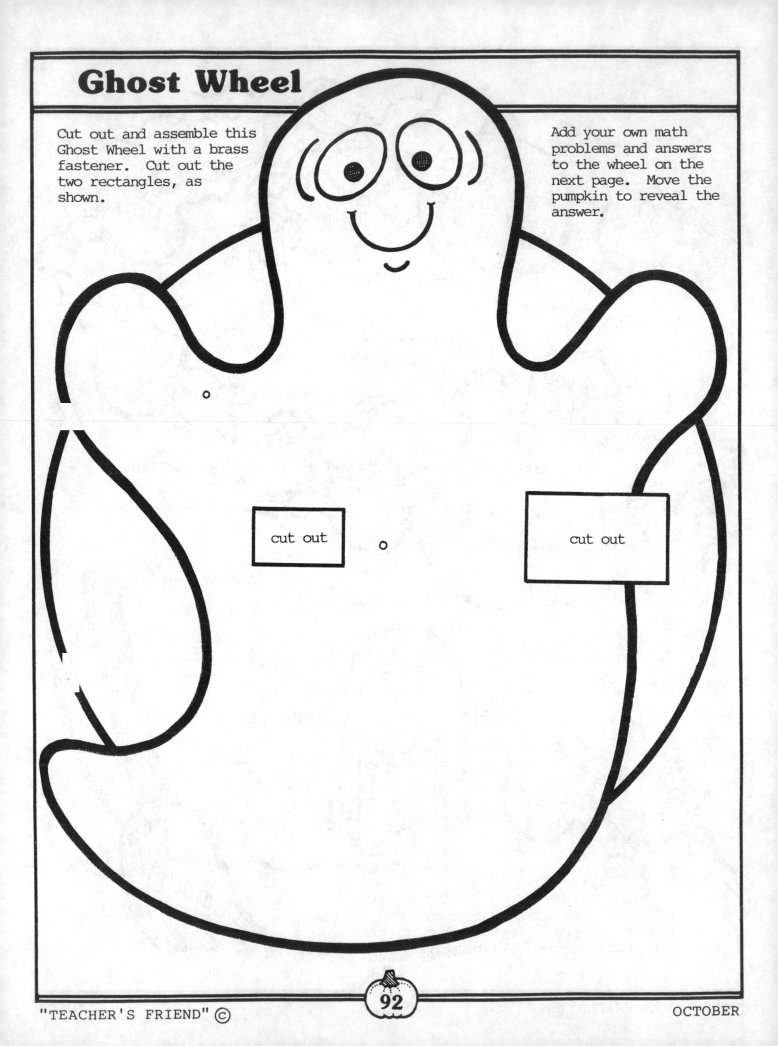

cut out

cut out

OCTOBER

Make one Ghost Wheel for each child in class. They will love learning their multiplication tables this fun way.

7 ○ 5+2

Halloween Safety Tips

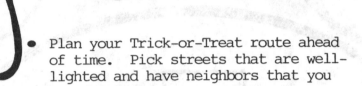

- Plan your Trick-or-Treat route ahead of time. Pick streets that are well-lighted and have neighbors that you know.

- Take a parent, or older sister or brother with you Trick-or-Treating. If someone older cannot go with you, Trick-or-Treat with a group.

- Trick-or-Treat when it is still light outside, if possible.

- Wear a costume that makes it easy for you to walk and can be seen after dark.

- Carry a flashlight and use reflective tape on your costume so people driving cars can see you.

- If you wear a mask, take it off before crossing streets. If possible, wear make-up instead of a mask.

- Cross only at corners. Never cross the street between parked cars or in the middle of a busy block.

- If there are no sidewalks, walk facing the traffic to make sure you can see the cars.

- Do not eat your candy until you get home and an adult can check it over for safety.

OCTOBER

Pumpkin   Puppet

Cut this pumpkin puppet pattern from construc- tion paper. Glue the pieces to a small paper lunch bag.

Creative Kettle Bones

THE INGREDIENTS FOR A MAGIC POTION ARE....

THE BEST HALLOWEEN COSTUME I EVER SAW WAS....

I KNOW THE HOUSE ON THE CORNER IS HAUNTED BECAUSE....

THIS MORNING ON THE WAY TO SCHOOL I FOUND A MAGIC RING....

LAST NIGHT AS I WAS PASSING THE GRAVEYARD....

Enlarge this witch's kettle on black butcher paper and display on the class bulletin board. Children can pull a bone from the kettle and write a creative story. Copy extra bones on white construction paper and have students write their own ideas for spooky stories.

Bat Pattern

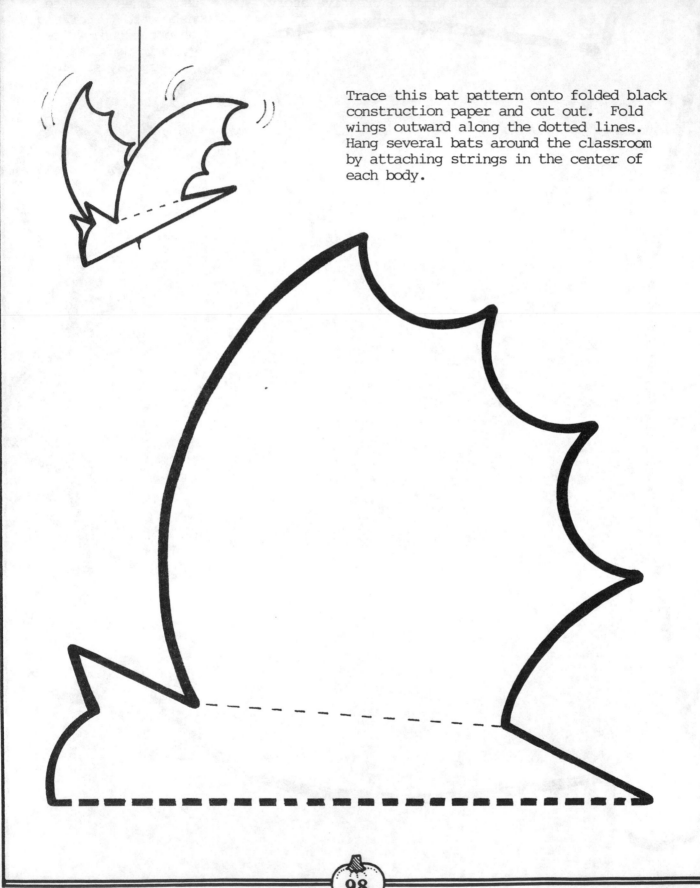

Trace this bat pattern onto folded black construction paper and cut out. Fold wings outward along the dotted lines. Hang several bats around the classroom by attaching strings in the center of each body.

OCTOBER

Spider Pattern

Trace this spider pattern onto black construction paper and cut out. Fold the legs inward along the dotted lines. Add sequins for eyes if you wish. Set the spider on a table top or hang by a string in the classroom.

Epitaphs

R.I.P.

Develop creative writing skills by having
students write funny epitaphs.

Harvest Time

Bulletin Boards

GHOST WRITERS

Have students write "ghostly" stories on white paper ghost cut-outs. Display them on the class bulletin board omitting each author's name. Children will have fun guessing which story was written by which "ghost" writer.

HARVEST OF GOOD WORK

Children will enjoy collecting fall leaves for this autumn bulletin board. Pin the real leaves around the board and cut paper leaves for the good work papers. Write the owners' names on the paper leaves with colored markers.

FANG-TASTIC!

Take the "bite" out of school work by displaying Dracula on the class bulletin board. Cover the board with black paper. Place Dracula's face and hands above the board, as shown. Children will be eager to see their papers displayed in such a "fang-tastic!" way.

and more....

OUR READING PATCH

Display a large orange pumpkin for each student on the class bulletin board. As assignments are completed or stories read, the students add eyes, noses and mouths to their pumpkins which quickly turn into jack-o'-lanterns.

SPOOKY MURAL

Everyone in class will love adding their own touches to a "spooky" mural. Cover the board with black paper and have children add cut paper haunted houses and flying ghosts. Colored chalk can be used to add details.

WHICH IS WITCH

Students will love studying homonyms with this clever bulletin board. Display a large Halloween witch in one corner. Write different homonyms on strips of colored paper and place them around the board. Children can match up the words when work is completed.

FIREPROOF YOUR HOME

- SMOKE DETECTORS
- FIRE EXTINGUISHER
- CORDS IN GOOD SHAPE
- OUTLETS NOT OVERLOADED
- NO LOOSE CLOTHES WHILE COOKING
- GASOLINE KEPT PROPERLY
- HEATER KEPT AWAY FROM DRAPES
- KEEP MATCHES FROM CHILDREN

FIREPROOF YOUR HOME

Instruct students on the value of fire prevention with the help of this fire safety bulletin board. After class discussion, list items that should be checked to insure a fire safe home. Display this list on the board along with a cut-out paper match or fire extinguisher.

WHOOOOOOO KNOWS

Enlarge this "wise" owl onto poster board and display in the center of a bulletin board. Cut pictures of famous people and places from magazines and periodicals and arrange them around the owl. Ask students to identify each picture and award the student with the most correct answers.

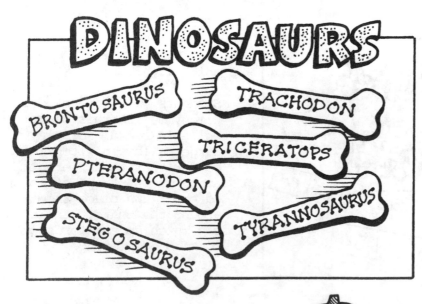

DINOSAURS

BRONTOSAURUS
TRACHODON
TRICERATOPS
PTERANODON
TYRANNOSAURUS
STEGOSAURUS

BONE UP ON DINOSAURS

Display dinosaur names on large paper bones cut from white construction paper. Students can list dinosaur facts under the names along with drawings of each dinosaur.

SPOOKY HEADLINES

Tear letters from white paper for a "spooky" effect. Letters can also be cut from rolled cotton or crumpled pieces of plastic wrap.

ROAD MAP LETTERS

Large letters cut from old road maps will add interest to a bulletin board on mapping skills.

NAME THAT TUNE

Cut headline letters from old sheet music or pages from discarded song books.

STYROFOAM HEADLINES

Cut letters from styrofoam sheets. This is a great way to announce the coming of "Winter" or a unit on "Alaska."

CURRENT EVENTS

Get students' attention by display-ing headlines cut from real head-lines or from classified ad pages.

FEATHERED FRIENDS

A bulletin board announcing a unit on birds will literally jump off the wall with the letters written in real feathers.

RED, WHITE AND BLUE

Celebrate patriotic themes by cutting letters from red, white and blue strip-ed wrapping paper.

OCTOBER

Ghost Writing

Witch and
Ghost

Fang-tastic

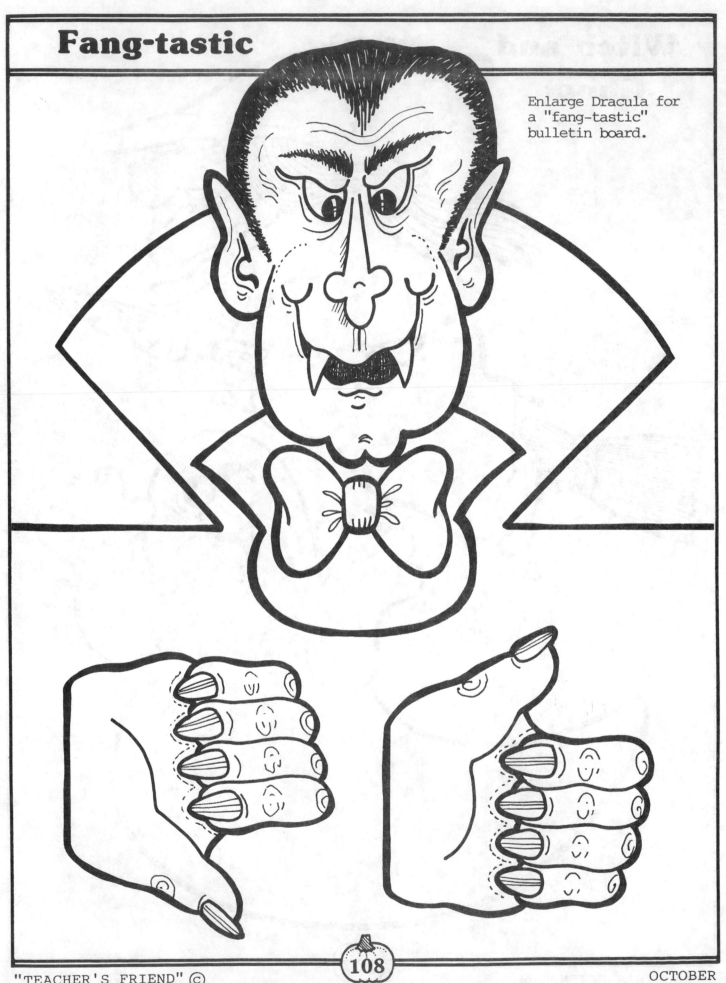

Enlarge Dracula for a "fang-tastic" bulletin board.

OCTOBER

Haunted House

Enlarge this haunted house for a spooky bulletin board display. Children can add the finishing touches, including pumpkins, ghosts and other scary characters at the windows.

You might like to add your own math problems. Have your students solve the problems and color the picture.

OCTOBER

Notes

Answer Key

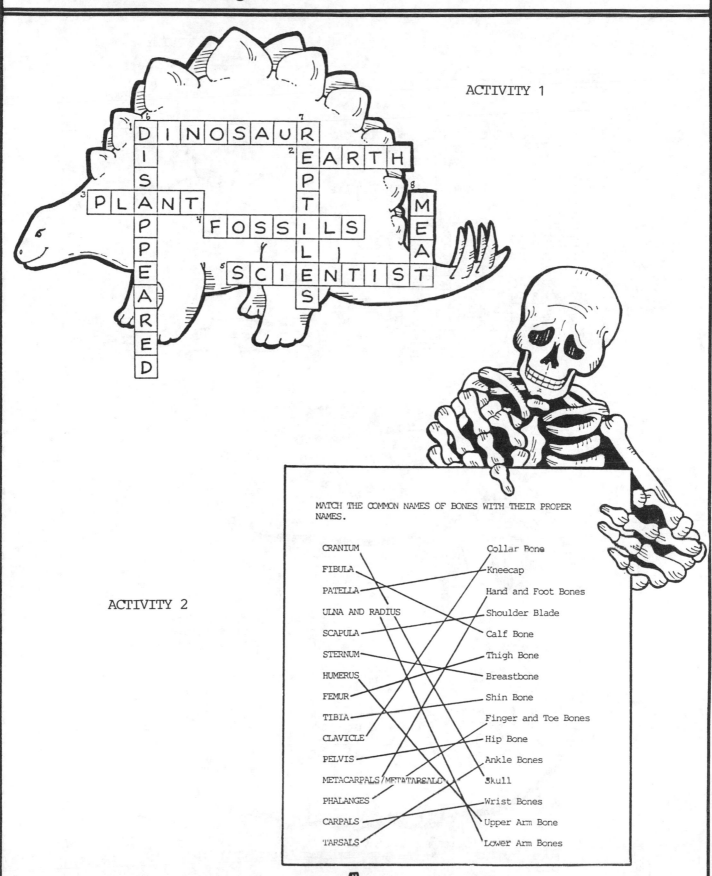

ACTIVITY 1

Crossword (answers):
- 1 DISAPPEARED
- 6 DINOSAUR
- 7 REPTILES
- 2 EARTH
- 3 PLANT
- 8 MEAT
- 4 FOSSILS
- 5 SCIENTIST

ACTIVITY 2

MATCH THE COMMON NAMES OF BONES WITH THEIR PROPER NAMES.

CRANIUM	Collar Bone
FIBULA	Kneecap
PATELLA	Hand and Foot Bones
ULNA AND RADIUS	Shoulder Blade
SCAPULA	Calf Bone
STERNUM	Thigh Bone
HUMERUS	Breastbone
FEMUR	Shin Bone
TIBIA	Finger and Toe Bones
CLAVICLE	Hip Bone
PELVIS	Ankle Bones
METACARPALS / METATARSALS	Skull
PHALANGES	Wrist Bones
CARPALS	Upper Arm Bone
TARSALS	Lower Arm Bones

OCTOBER

Answer Key

FIND THESE WORDS IN THE PUZZLE BELOW: COLUMBUS, NIÑA, PINTA, SANTA MARIA, SPAIN, SAN SALVADOR, NEW WORLD, AMERICA, KING FERDINAND, QUEEN ISABELLA

```
D V B H Y U J K O L M N H G V B H F R T Y
C O L U M B U S S E R T G Y H U J K I L P
W E R T G Y H P D C V B Q S E R T Y U I P
Z C V F G T H A S W R T U F G H Y U J M N
C F G R T B N I F R T Y E D R Y H J P S Q
S C V B G F D N R T Y H E C O L K I I N G
A M E T Y F E B C D R W N Q X C V T N H U
N E S A N T A M A R I A I F V B G T T D R
S W E T Y G H U I J K Y S D R T Y E A V F
B G T Y U J H F G T V B A M E R I C A T U
W E R T G D V F H F T R B W T Y U P I B N
Q U E F T G H K I N G F E R D I N A N D R
D C V G H B G F V F D S L S R T G Y T R E
D N E W W O R L D F T E L F R T Y G F R E
F B V C D S A N S A L V A D O R F T Y H U
S D F G T Y H U J N B V C X Z D R T G D R
S R V B N M K J G F D N I Ñ A S E F Y H O
```

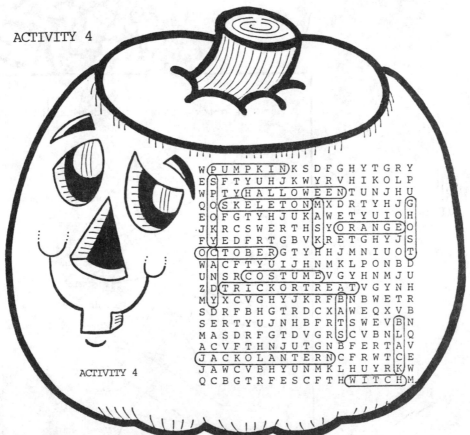

ACTIVITY 4

```
W P U M P K I N K S D F G H Y T G R Y
E S F T Y U H J K W Y R V H I K O L P
W P T Y H A L L O W E E N T U N J H U
Q O S K E L E T O N M X D R T Y H J G
E O F G T Y H J U K A W E T Y U I O H
E J K R C S W E R T H S Y O R A N G E O
F Y E D F R T G B V K R E T G H Y J S
O C T O B E R G T Y H H J M N I U O T
W A C F T Y U I J H N M K L P O N B D
U N S R C O S T U M E V G Y H N M J U
Z D T R I C K O R T R E A T V G Y N H
M Y X C V G H Y J K R F B N B W E T R
S D R F B H G T R D C X A W E Q X V B
S E R T Y U J N H B F R T S W E V B N
M A S D R F G T D V G R S C V B N L A
A C V F T H N J U T G N B F E R T A C
J A C K O L A N T E R N C F R W T C E
J A W C V B H Y U N M K L H U Y R K W
Q C B G T R F E S C F T H W I T C H M
```

FIND THESE HIDDEN WORDS: CANDY, COSTUME, MASK, JACK O' LANTERN, ORANGE, BLACK, SKELETON, SPOOKY, TRICK OR TREAT, BATS, GHOST, WITCH, PUMPKIN, HALLOWEEN, OCTOBER.